Effective Remote Teams

Building for the Web

Carleton DiLeo
Jennifer Reyes

Apress®

Effective Remote Teams: Building for the Web

Carleton DiLeo
Denver, CO, USA

Jennifer Reyes
Denver, CO, USA

ISBN-13 (pbk): 979-8-8688-1302-3
https://doi.org/10.1007/979-8-8688-1303-0

ISBN-13 (electronic): 979-8-8688-1303-0

Managing Director, Apress Media LLC: Welmoed Spahr
Acquisitions Editor: Shivangi Ramachandran
Development Editor: James Markham
Editorial Assistant: Jessica Vakili
Copy Editor: Kim Burton

Cover designed by eStudioCalamar

Distributed to the book trade worldwide by Springer Science+Business Media New York, 1 New York Plaza, Suite 4600, New York, NY 10004-1562, USA. Phone 1-800-SPRINGER, fax (201) 348-4505, e-mail orders-ny@springer-sbm.com, or visit www.springeronline.com. Apress Media, LLC is a California LLC and the sole member (owner) is Springer Science + Business Media Finance Inc (SSBM Finance Inc). SSBM Finance Inc is a **Delaware** corporation.

For information on translations, please e-mail booktranslations@springernature.com; for reprint, paperback, or audio rights, please e-mail bookpermissions@springernature.com.

Apress titles may be purchased in bulk for academic, corporate, or promotional use. eBook versions and licenses are also available for most titles. For more information, reference our Print and eBook Bulk Sales web page at http://www.apress.com/bulk-sales.

Any source code or other supplementary material referenced by the author in this book is available to readers on GitHub. For more detailed information, please visit https://www.apress.com/gp/services/source-code.

If disposing of this product, please recycle the paper

To my sister for always believing in me and to my nieces and nephews for always making me want to strive for more
—Carleton DiLeo

To Madison and Elisabeth, the two people in my life that always make me want to do better
—Jennifer Reyes

Table of Contents

About the Authors

Carleton DiLeo is a software developer with 20 years of experience working in everything from VR to web development. He went 100 percent remote in 2016 and has been responsible for building remote teams from the ground up, as well as helping existing teams improve their remote setup. He is currently a remote principal software engineer building robust, scalable systems.

Jennifer Reyes is a software engineer who spends most of her time building robust backend solutions across several web application frameworks. She spent 13 years working with Ruby on Rails before diving into PHP's Laravel and Python's Django. With over 12 years of remote work experience, Jennifer understands and advocates for clear communication, a good work-life balance, and transparency for every team. She's currently a remote staff engineer. When she's not writing code, you can find her exploring new coffee shops and collecting journals.

Acknowledgments

To the companies that have allowed us to work remotely throughout our career: thank you for letting us shape your remote culture and learn to lead with heart and for giving us the ability to do what we love while still spending time with our families.

Thank you to the Apress team, which believed in this book and helped us through its writing process.

Introduction

Plenty of books will teach you how to run a software team. Each presents a unique methodology, which, when used correctly, can provide excellent results. The issue is these books don't account for the unique challenges of working remotely. That's because remote teams weren't commonplace until a few years ago.

Fast-forward to the present, and you'll find the industry has changed. Developers can work from anywhere and switch companies without uprooting their lives. With more and more developers making the jump to remote work, we felt the need for a book that focused on the unique challenges of the new environment.

Why We Wrote This Book

Why us? What makes us, the authors, qualified to write this book? Individually, we each have over a decade of remote work experience. Carleton has experience building remote teams from the ground up, and Jennifer has worked with several existing remote teams to improve efficiency and productivity. We have a lot of experience to pull from. The ideas in this book aren't theory; both authors have put them into practice and have adapted in-person skills to work in a remote environment. On this decade-long journey, we tweaked our approach and expanded our knowledge, improving and sharing with each other until we reached a consensus.

This book is the culmination of that work and an opportunity to share what we've learned. You will learn from our mistakes, skip all the headaches, and start benefiting from everything remote development has to offer.

You will learn that adopting a remote-first approach is not only a viable option for building software but, in many ways, an optimal approach that every company, new or old, should consider. As more people move to full remote, it becomes the inevitable future of the field.

Who This Book Is For

We wrote this book for the co-founders responsible for building a team to execute the company's vision. It is for the engineering manager who needs to understand how their teams will produce quality code while located in different physical spaces. Finally, we created this book for the team lead, who must deal with the everyday challenges of leading, ensuring that collaboration and throughput are always high.

This book was written for readers who are starting from the ground up. There is no team or a single line of code. There is only an idea for a product, a bit of VC funding, and the excitement to dive in and get started.

You are interested in remote development because it seems like the right fit, and you're excited about the potential. You're onboard after hearing promises of a bigger talent pool to hire from, and you saved expenses by not having to sign a multiyear contract. Plus, you will finally get to use that home office you set up, but never used.

The problem is that you've never run a remote team before. You've heard the success stories of teams going remote, eliminating expenses, and increasing productivity. You've equally heard horror stories about remote teams' productivity grinding to a halt and companies slowly failing under the weight of unfinished work.

These stories haunt you more than you care to admit. You lose sleep over how to stop this from being you. Okay, maybe it's not this dire, but you wouldn't mind getting the benefits of remote teams while avoiding the pitfalls. This book is your guide to get you there.

What if you already have an in-person team you'd like to transition to remote? Or even a remote team that isn't operating as well as you'd hoped? You can still gain a lot from this book. You'll be able to compare your current processes to the ones we outlined and pick and choose how to implement them.

You might decide that your remote team is already running smoothly, in which case, you should give yourself a pat on the back.

How This Book Is Organized

We start by defining the qualities of an ineffective, remote team because knowing what not to do is just as important as knowing what works. We compare the bad with the good. We analyze each aspect of software development and provide the tools and processes you need to build a productive remote team.

We break down this process into three steps: The Setup, The Work, and Keeping It Together. Each section focuses on different stages of building a team and provides options you can use now and what to consider for the future. We outline the steps you will perform at each part of the journey. Most importantly, we work toward building a proactive mindset that prepares for trouble rather than only reacting to it, giving you the control you need to run a successful business.

The Setup describes what to do before hiring your first developer or committing a single code line. We lay the groundwork for your team to work effectively now and in the future. After completing this part, you will have what you need to start hiring and begin development.

The Work teaches you the skills you need to manage the day-to-day operations. You learn how to deal with the ups and downs of remote life. You develop the skills to handle problems gracefully and, with preparation, prevent future catastrophes before they happen. We teach you how to structure your team to keep you sane and your developers productive.

INTRODUCTION

Keeping It Together outlines a plan to minimize turnover while keeping your engineers happy and productive. Our goal is to see your teams grow without all the growing pains. Even though they may be in different parts of the world, we aim to foster a sense of connection and engagement that leads to a shared vision with the company, inspiring and motivating your team members.

PART I

Introduction

CHAPTER 1

Remote Work is the Future

Modern web application frameworks have made transitioning from the initial idea to the working prototype a breeze. People can set up a CRM, e-commerce store, or a business website with minimal programming experience. And if you believe all the boot camps, tutorials, and video courses advertised online, anyone can learn to code in weeks or even minutes. It's only a matter of having the time or the money to do it. Then why do 90% of startups fail?[1]

It's because it takes a lot of work to make the leap from a working prototype to a full-fledged web application with paying users and a loyal customer base. This chapter takes a closer look at this struggle of building software and the tools that have become available over the years. We discuss the shift from in-person working to remote development and how it's changing the software development landscape.

---

[1] `https://www.failory.com/blog/startup-failure-rate`: Startups have a 90% failure rate.

© Carleton DiLeo, Jennifer Reyes 2025
C. DiLeo and J. Reyes, *Effective Remote Teams*,
https://doi.org/10.1007/979-8-8688-1303-0_1

Building Web Applications Is Hard

For a software company to be successful, it needs the following traits: technical expertise, focus and efficiency, and highly collaborative teams. Without them, problems won't take long to start piling up, drowning the company and possibly forcing it to close its doors.

As monthly user counts grow, the demand for newer and better features escalates. The entry of new companies into our space necessitates innovation to stand out in a competitive market. In turn, our app must grow in complexity and scope, a natural progression in our field, which leads to the expansion of our engineering team.

But bigger isn't always better in software development. Throwing more bodies at a codebase doesn't equate to higher productivity. If it were that simple, anyone could find a bunch of talented developers and rent an office, and the software would start flowing from their fingertips, right? No. Unfortunately, it's not that simple. When you add more people to a team, overhead increases. The increased overhead amplifies the complexity of many aspects of running the team. Eventually, there will be a point where you will see diminishing returns for each new hire.

Hopefully, we haven't scared you off from reading further. Over the years, a lot of work has been done to address these problems.

- Agile makes it easier to fail quickly and recover without significant financial ramifications.

- Modern computer languages and frameworks let us do more with less.

- Practices like test-driven development create a workflow that allows developers to write code without fear of code regressions.

- Collaborative online tools make it easy for teams to organize code, deploy software, and communicate, no matter where they are.

These welcome changes have enabled our industry to adapt to a dramatic shift in how we build software. Without even knowing it, we enabled our workforce to finally break the need for an office and work remotely, setting us up for what was to come.

The Paradigm Shift

A few years ago, the development world underwent a dramatic paradigm shift. A global pandemic forced companies to move from the physical work environment to a remote one (Figure 1-1).

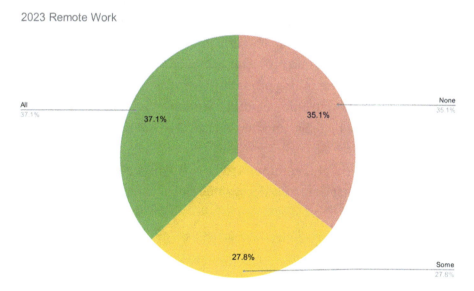

Figure 1-1. *Remote work in 2023*

This change, which initially seemed like a temporary solution, has now evolved into a promising new way to work. The change stuck even after people started returning to the office. Some companies adopted hybrid work policies, and some ditched the office entirely in favor of a fully remote workforce.

According to the Bureau of Labor Statistics, as of 2023, 37.1% of the people in the "Computer and Mathematical" field are fully remote. Also, an additional 27.8% work at least a few hours remotely each week.[2] This marks a substantial change from the 2010 report released by GetApp, which indicated that only 9.5% of the United States workforce reported working remotely[3].

The shift to remote work happened so fast and was so overreaching in the technology field that having a flexible working policy has become the expectation rather than the exception. Some companies resisted the change and forced workers to return to a physical office. The response among engineers was not positive. Companies that required employees to be in the office lost good engineers to others who embraced flexibility.

For the ones that stuck with it, remote work introduced new hurdles to overcome. Teams ran into problems like poor communication, security policies not extending properly to home offices, and a lack of understanding of how to enforce normal working hours. As a result, productivity took a huge hit, and managers forced employees back into the office.

However, some teams continued to thrive in this new world of remote work. But why? What were they doing differently?

---

[2] https://www.bls.gov/opub/ted/2023/about-1-in-3-workers-in-management-professional-and-related-occupations-teleworked-november-2023.htm 64.9% work some remote hours while 37.1% work fully remote.

[3] https://www.getapp.com/resources/decade-in-tech/#remote-work-nearly-quadrupled-in-the-last-decade Remote work quadrupled in the past decade. People who work at least one day a work remotely went from 9.5% in 2010 to 36% in 2020.

The Keys to Success

Successful development teams that embraced remote work already valued self-direction, efficiency, and simple yet impactful solutions. They demonstrated adaptability, streamlining their processes to accommodate asynchronous communication and maintaining productivity despite not being co-located. Their success serves as an example of how remote work can bring positive changes to organizations and foster a more productive team.

In fact, remote teams have the potential to outperform in-person ones. It's hard to believe, but it is possible. That's because building remote teams forces us to critically examine all aspects of the software development process. We must excel at time management and improve communication with co-workers.

Instead of relying on the crutches of in-person interactions, we must elevate every aspect of our software pipeline and make it a well-oiled machine that functions without constant maintenance. Anything less means your developers will be sitting on their hands with nothing to do, wasting company money as their interest in their jobs wanes.

Summary

This chapter discussed how the industry shift from in-person to remote working has changed how we build web applications. It covered the rise of cloud-based online services, which has made the transition to remote work much more accessible. Finally, it outlined how adopting remote working allows a flexible and productive team. The next chapter explains how to identify the symptoms of a poorly run remote team.

CHAPTER 2

Symptoms of a Dysfunctional Remote Team

Let's make something clear before we start: no one sets out to run a remote team poorly. Small budgets and indecisive top-level leadership can make smoothly running any team nearly impossible. Managing remote developers isn't easy, even when everything is set up for success. Communication and collaboration that can be effortless for in-person teams are a struggle when working remotely due to distance and differing schedules.

Spotting these problems isn't always easy. This chapter discusses the symptoms of an ineffective remote team. It examines each in detail, providing examples so you have a clear picture. If you already have a remote team, you might recognize some of these problems and understand the struggle they create. Let's start with a story.

© Carleton DiLeo, Jennifer Reyes 2025
C. DiLeo and J. Reyes, *Effective Remote Teams*,
https://doi.org/10.1007/979-8-8688-1303-0_2

A Story: The Perils of a Dysfunctional Remote Team

The alarm goes off on Betty's nightstand. A hand fumbles for a phone, which falls end over end to the floor and slides under the bed. It's 8 a.m. on Monday, and work is inevitable. She gets up and moves through her morning routine, willing her eyes to stay open and trying not to spill coffee on her white shirt.

When she strolls into her home office, the wall clock reads 9 a.m. Her laptop boots and notifications start filling the top-right corner of the screen. Last night, the site went down again. The developers, unfortunate enough to be online when it happened, were still online, scrambling to locate the source.

Betty checked her calendar and noticed the daily scrum call had been canceled for the second day in a row. Now she would have to wait another day to get answers to blocking issues for her task, which is already two weeks late. Hopefully, no one will notice since the team has missed the last few milestones.

Betty didn't have access to the cloud servers; getting access was still on her manager's to-do list, so she could do nothing to help. She looked at the backlog and couldn't find a new task fleshed out enough to work on. None of the tasks were well written, and it was unclear what the product managers wanted. Betty could already feel the wave of dread wash over her. It looked like another day of browsing the web and doing "research."

Her phone chimed. She picked it up and saw a message. It was from the recruiter who'd been trying to reach Betty for months. This was an automated follow-up, asking if now was a good time to discuss a new job opportunity.

She usually ignored the messages, but today, her gaze lingered on the message, reviewing the job description. Finally, she typed a one-word reply: YES.

Our short story illustrates the woes of a developer in a dysfunctional remote team. It's Monday, and the team is already in full meltdown. Our developer, Betty, is helpless as the chaos unfolds.

Let's begin looking at the different symptoms of an ineffective remote team.

Problematic Backlog

Backlogs represent an application's overall potential. They should be well-defined and filled with tasks outlining improvements, new ideas, and bug fixes. A healthy backlog is a roadmap for what your application will become. It is always evolving and changing.

This is because the needs of the people who use our application aren't fixed. The more they use and rely on an application, the more they uncover bugs or think of new features. It's precisely the kind of behavior we want. Without it, their engagement fizzles out, and user activity dwindles.

If your backlog isn't healthy, this can be an issue for your team. This means there is either insufficient work to support the current team size or a problem somewhere else in the pipeline with defining tasks. Either way, this lack of work results in developers sitting on their hands doing nothing.

Since remote teams tend to work different hours and aren't located in the same physical space, asking for help isn't always an option. Even with these roadblocks, some developers will find a way to keep busy, but we shouldn't rely on this.

What does a problematic backlog look like, and how can you tell if you have one? Let's examine some ways to determine this.

Too Few Tasks

The first issue might seem obvious, but it is the easiest to spot. A backlog with only a week or two of planned work is too little for a team. It tells us that there is no long-term vision for the product. Also, one to two weeks of tasks doesn't provide enough buffer. If you aren't paying attention, the team might burn through that work faster than expected, leaving them with nothing to work on.

When that happens, the software team will meet for a planning meeting and find an empty backlog. Now, the team must think of new work to keep busy. Planning a sprint under pressure doesn't usually result in well-defined tasks. These hastily defined tasks can cause problems for the current sprint and problems that might not be felt until much later.

Poorly Defined Tasks

Sometimes, even when your backlog is overflowing, it can still be unhealthy. Just because there is a lot of work to do doesn't mean proper planning went into defining that work.

When we look at our backlog, each task must be clearly written and prioritized based on its importance and dependencies. A task should have a description, acceptance criteria, and any additional information the developer should consider. Without this, even the most senior developer could be left scratching their head.

When tasks are unclear, developers may make incorrect assumptions, leading to wasted time. Depending on your workflow, the feature could make it to production without being caught. User complaints or the product person randomly stumbling upon the feature might be the only way the developer finds out something is wrong. Additionally, the developer will need to sync with the task's stakeholders to pry the information out of them. And when you're remote, tracking down people can take time. When this issue is combined with insufficient defined work, the result is a developer with nothing to do.

Let's look at some examples of poorly defined tasks.

A Closer Look

In this example, a product person works at an e-commerce site. They've been brainstorming ways to improve the admin tools used to manage the company's products. Many of the customer service representatives complained that it was hard to locate problem orders. They have to scroll and page through hundreds of orders to find the one they need. A search would be a significant improvement.

The product person fires up their browser, loads the team's project management tool, and creates an Order Search task with the following description.

> *Add a search to the order page that lets the user search all orders.*

> *Satisfied, they sign off for the week and go for their afternoon walk. A developer picks up the task on Monday and deploys it later that week.*

One day, the product manager receives an email asking when the order search will be done. Confused, the product manager checks the customer service admin tool and is unable to find the new search feature. They contact the developer who worked on the task and ask why it was closed if the new search wasn't completed. The defensive developer says it was completed. The order search functionality was added to the customer order page. They thought the task was odd, but it was approved. Allowing customers to search for orders that weren't theirs seemed like a security risk, but they couldn't get a hold of anyone, so they went ahead with the change.

As you can see, the product person's mistake of not specifying *what user* requested the search feature caused the developer to assume incorrectly. A peer review or another pass on the task would have caught the issue.

Clearly defined tasks are essential. Now, this example may be far-fetched. A seasoned engineer should catch the problem during peer review. However, it's not inconceivable that poorly defined tasks could lead to serious issues with the application.

Team Conflicts

Next, let's discuss team conflicts. This occurs when two or more developers work on overlapping parts of the application. When this happens, the result is merge conflicts, duplicated work, and problems deploying. Conflicts are the result of an inadequately planned backlog. Tasks should be ordered by dependency or reworked to avoid overlap. If the product team doesn't take the time to do this, the development team will face problems. If you notice your team is constantly clashing when work starts, you may have a problematic backlog.

Slow Velocity

Getting the most out of an employee is not unique to software development. Any company, big or small, wants everyone to be as productive as possible. Productive people make the company money. It also keeps employees motivated and happy since their skills and time aren't being wasted. After all, we all work to earn a living, but no one wants to feel like they're just trading their time for a salary. It feels good when our efforts build toward an end goal that customers find worthwhile enough to spend their money on.

This feeling of progress is everything to someone who writes software for a living. It's what drives us to do what we do. We want to solve a problem and move on to the next one with minimal resistance.

That brings us to our second symptom of a bad remote team: slow velocity. If a remote team has slow velocity, it isn't getting much done. It is often blocked or takes much longer than it should to finish a task. How do you tell if your team's velocity is slow? Let's look at different signs you can look for.

Incorrect Estimates

Sprint planning meetings allow a team to understand what everyone will be working on. The structure of these meetings can vary widely between companies or even between different teams within the same organization. One thing you can count on is that they provide critical insight into how the team is functioning.

Imagine it's Monday morning, and everyone has joined the sprint planning meeting. As the manager, you've requested each developer to provide a status update. This includes tasks completed during the last sprint as well as current work. As they are sharing, you notice something is wrong. Many tasks estimated to take a day have taken the entire week, and some tasks estimated to take a week are still ongoing. It's not just one developer having issues; most developers have overshot their original estimate significantly.

What troubles you the most is that this isn't an isolated occurrence. Most weekly syncs follow a similar path. You know that each person is trying their hardest to get work done. In fact, many have reported working late multiple nights and on the weekend.

If a team finds that estimates rarely match the actual time to complete the task, deeper issues are likely present, such as poor task definition, improper planning, and conflicts. These issues can cause a slowdown and, in the worst case, cause your team to sit on their hands, waiting for help.

For a remote team, these problems are amplified due to poor communication. People may miss important messages simply because their communication tools weren't configured properly. These communication breakdowns slow progress, causing tasks to be late. When this happens, frustrated users will let you know. That brings us to our next indication of slow velocity.

Constant Update Requests

If you've noticed your team is moving slowly, chances are others have too. If your company has more than a handful of people, the development team's work will probably affect their work.

Often, a dev team has external and internal users. External users are anyone outside of your organization that uses the application. Internal users are employees of your company. They may use the app via a special admin interface. Like your external users, they'll want bugs promptly fixed and new features released regularly.

When your team falls behind, these users will start asking questions. They will want to know how long until a critical bug is fixed or the new feature blocking a sales deal is deployed. If this happens often, the CEO will become aware and want to know what could be done to unblock the rest of the company.

In summary, if the non-technical staff starts asking questions or complaining about how long it takes to implement new features or resolve bugs, then that is a problem. And if the CEO starts asking questions about progress, you're in big trouble.

Team Morale

Team morale is another thing to look for when determining whether you are experiencing velocity issues. This one isn't as obvious as the other indicators and largely depends on your team dynamic.

If your team is normally outspoken, you might notice a drop in opinions being voiced during meetings. When a meeting is finished, people will quickly drop off a call, never sticking around to chat or demonstrate what they are working on.

A morale drop is harder to identify if your team is more withdrawn. Problems might show up on one-on-one calls. You may notice that much of your time together is focused on topics other than personal growth. You will talk about problems with team dynamics, workflow, and other issues impeding the developer from completing their work. The next section explains how a slow ramp-up for new hires can signify a dysfunctional remote team.

Slow Ramp-up

Growing a team is a critical part of a healthy company. If that company is successful, the demand for a software team to deliver new features and alter the system to handle increased load will eventually become too much. When this happens, the team needs to bring on new people. Those new developers need to become productive as soon as possible. If that doesn't happen, this can cause a serious strain on the team.

Let's start with an example of a team with slow ramp-up from the perspective of the new hire and the hiring manager.

A Story: A New Hire

Sheena recently gave her two-week notice only after four months on the team. Alice, an engineering manager, was interviewing candidates for Sheena's vacant position. Alice and her team interviewed Charlie, who seemed like an ideal candidate. He knew the technology stack and had worked in the industry before. There were no red flags, and he had a positive outlook.

Charlie

The team welcomes Charlie as the newest engineer. His first day going through the HR onboarding process goes smoothly. Alice and the team take some time during sync to get to know Charlie and his background. He's given access to the code and the different staging environments. All in all, Charlie is off to a great start.

He's told to attend sprint planning tomorrow, so he pokes around the application to get an idea of its core functionality. He continues by reviewing old PRs, which gives him a sense of the features he will be working on and the problems he will address. Additionally, he's able to see the type of feedback his peers give and gains an understanding of the team dynamic.

During his first sprint planning, he listened attentively and followed along with the tasks that were pulled into the sprint. He noticed that tasks are assigned based on area expertise and that several bugs appeared in this week's sprint. Charlie is assigned three tasks.

- Complete local environment setup.

- Fix a broken test.

- Add filtering to an internal API that's consumed by two different services.

Charlie ended his day feeling positive. The next day, he opened the ReadMe within the codebase and attempted to set up his local environment. He navigated to the relevant section and followed the directions for setting up his local instance.

He gets stuck in the process and tries to ask a co-worker for assistance. No one's online. He checks the calendar and sees that most of his team won't be online for another three hours. He fires off a calendar invite for a pairing session to see if he can get through this hump.

Without wanting to waste his day, Charlie continues looking through PRs and studying the code. He even combs through the backlog to see if there are any low-priority tasks that he could take on.

It's now noon for Charlie, and he grabs lunch. While eating, he is notified that his meeting invite has been declined. Charlie pings a co-worker, who is busy but suggests he contact Cynthia. But Cynthia works async in the morning and then jumps back online in the evening. So, Charlie asks his manager if there's anyone available to help him with his environment setup, and his manager refers him to the ReadMe within the codebase. Feeling frustrated and defeated, Charlie ends his day early.

Thankfully, the next day, Charlie is able to get his environment working. He moves on to his next task: fixing the broken test. And when he runs the test suite, several unrelated tests are failing. Searching through the errors, he deduces that he's missing access to an Amazon Web Services (AWS) service. Again, he asks his manager, who then directs him to someone in DevOps. He's informed that this will take a few days.

He's feeling antsy about not contributing to the codebase yet, so Charlie decides to book a meeting with Cynthia, even though it's outside his normal working hours. This way, he can shadow her on a task and better understand the workflow used to complete tasks.

When he finally gains access to the AWS service, he can run the test and resolve the issue. But now it's Monday, and the next sprint is about to start.

This cycle of getting assigned tasks, being unable to complete them, and feeling frustrated becomes an unfortunate pattern. Charlie brings up the issues with his team. He tells them about the lack of onboarding process, documentation, access to team members, and access to platform services during retrospectives. However, no one else seems to be having these issues.

Fast-forward to the end of Charlie's first quarter. It's been three months, and he's having his first real one-on-one meeting with Alice. She suggests that maybe this isn't the right fit for Charlie and that she expected more, given that he took on a senior software engineering role. Since he is still on probation, the company has decided to let Charlie go.

Alice

Alice was genuinely surprised when things weren't working out with Charlie. She had expected that he would be able to integrate smoothly with the team and increase the team's productivity. However, that wasn't the case.

Instead, Alice felt Charlie was lacking. Alice could only assign Charlie a few story points each sprint because he would have too much carryover from the previous one. During Charlie's exit interview, Alice cited that he needed to improve his self-directed learning and take a more proactive problem-solving approach. In Alice's mind, these critiques were all merited.

Summary

Our story about Alice and her new hire, Charlie, illustrates how a bad onboarding process can affect a team's ability to bring on new people. When working remotely, this problem can go unnoticed until it's too late. Alice was blinded by her team's success and thought Charlie had everything he needed. After all, the team didn't have any major productivity issues. For Charlie, joining the new company was an experience of isolation and frustration. No matter how hard he tried, he could not overcome the barriers placed in front of him.

When bringing on new developers, failure to meet expectations for initial contributions or sprint velocity might indicate something wrong with your team's onboarding, not the new hire. It takes time and continuous effort to maintain a good onboarding process. Creating a ReadMe on GitHub when the project was started but never touching it again will end in headaches. We need to do more if we plan on growing the team. Next, let's consider how a reactive mindset can indicate an ineffectively run remote team.

Reactive Problem-Solving

Planning is key to a healthy team. The more you plan, the less likely you will encounter unforeseen problems. Of course, there is always the exception. No matter how much you try to avoid it, issues happen. They are a natural part of software development, but there is a tipping point where you can get overwhelmed by the unexpected. When this happens, you may feel like you can never get ahead of the problems and always wish you had more time. That time would be spent planning and organizing the future. If you find yourself in a situation like this, chances are you have become a reactive problem solver, only able to tackle your job one day at a time.

What is reactive problem-solving? It's a state of mind in which you create solutions as a reaction to a current problem. You aren't thinking about how your change will affect future work. Instead, you only fix what is broken or deliver what is needed to satisfy a request.

Let's look at an example. Say a WebKit-based browser visits your site and clicks the login button. No matter how many times they click the button, nothing happens. They send you a passionate email about how your buggy site is preventing them from performing the action they set out to do. Checking the delivery date, you see the email was sent last week, but you only see it now. It's been a hectic week dealing with problem after problem. You respond to the user and apologize for the inconvenience. Then, you create a bug in your bug-tracking system and assign it to a developer.

Later that day, a developer is assigned to the bug and they work to determine the cause. The problem ends up being a small snippet of code that uses a JavaScript feature unavailable in WebKit-based browsers. A fix is created and subsequently deployed to production. The user is notified, and the ticket is closed. No one checks if the other browsers your site supports are compatible with the change. That night, hundreds of emails poured into the support inbox, stating the fix broke the login button for all other major browsers. The emails sit until morning, waiting for the first unsuspecting developer to log in. This repeats until, finally, all problems are fixed and your team can move on to the next pressing issue.

This scenario describes a team in a reactive problem-solving loop. When this happens, it feels like nothing of value is getting done. You react to problems as they happen and do not allocate time to the work the company needs. Tasks are completed with the bare minimum effort and often incur technical debt.

This is not an ideal approach to building software. It degrades team morale and hurts your company's ability to grow. So, what type of mindset do you want? You want the opposite of a reactive mindset—a proactive one, which is covered in detail in the next chapter.

Constant Fire Fighting

How many times has your site gone down this week? How many emails have you received that were marked urgent and required immediate attention? If your answer is more than once, your application is in the first stages of becoming unstable. If you answered a number in the double digits, you are fully in a reactive problem-solving workflow.

System outages happen to all websites, but if it's normal for your site to go down once a week or, worse, once a day, that is a good indication that something is very wrong. If this sounds like you, you probably spend most of your time reacting to these issues to restore users' access. When your site constantly fails and loses the company money, it's hard to argue with upper management that you need time to refactor and rewrite portions of the application. They want the site back up and running soon to avoid lost revenue.

No Time for Refactoring

When we touch a piece of code, we should always aim to improve it, even if the improvement is minor. For example, say a developer adds functionality to an existing part of the code. The developer notices the code needs to be better organized and finds the variables challenging to understand. As part of the change, they moved a logical group of statements to a method and renamed a few variables to provide better context for the data it's storing. All these little changes eventually lead to an easier codebase for developers to work with.

In a reactive environment, there is no time to refactor. Pull requests make the necessary changes to complete the task. Developers will complain about piling technical debt and having no time to "do it right." As a manager, you will notice that tasks take longer with each passing week because developers are working with brittle code put in place to satisfy the requirements of a task from weeks ago.

Some tools can help measure overall code quality, but if you can't afford these tools, just listen to your developers. Developers inherently want to write good code. If they aren't able to, they will tell you why.

Projects Pushed Back

Projects can get delayed for various reasons. If a team constantly pushes back project deadlines, rarely finishing anywhere near the projected date, that may be a sign that the team is in reactive problem-solving mode. This is because a team in reactive mode only thinks in the moment.

Each task or problem is solved in haste without considering how it will affect future progress. As work is merged together, bugs and conflicts are uncovered. The project becomes a tangled mess of overlapping issues that must be untangled before release.

Some work might need to be redone, which further adds to delays. When working remotely, these problems can remain hidden until the end of the project.

Summary

This chapter looked at all the different ways running a remote team can go wrong. Problematic backlogs cause confusion and conflict among the team. Slow velocity makes our projects drag on forever. A slow ramp-up process for new developers means it may be a long time before they can contribute anything meaningful to the team. Finally, a reactive approach to problem-solving results in our team always playing catch-up rather than looking to the future.

The next chapter examines the specific traits that indicate a remote team is running smoothly.

CHAPTER 3

Effective Remote Teams

When a team is in sync, sprints fly by without issue, and projects are completed on time. Development becomes almost routine, and successful outcomes are expected. An effective remote team operates in a way that is the antithesis of the chaos described in the previous chapter. Like a well-oiled machine, it's what every team aspires to. But what are the aspects of an effective remote team that make it operate as smoothly as it does?

An effective team clearly defines each member's roles and responsibilities to ensure everyone knows what is expected of them. They have a proactive problem-solving mindset, which allows them to anticipate and address problems before they become roadblocks. Everyone on the team is empathic, allowing for peaceful navigation through interpersonal dynamics. Information is shared openly across all teams, creating a sense of transparency and trust.

Each of these aspects is key to a successful team. They are all covered in this chapter, but like in the previous chapter, let's start with a story that highlights the life of a developer on an effective remote team.

© Carleton DiLeo, Jennifer Reyes 2025
C. DiLeo and J. Reyes, *Effective Remote Teams*,
https://doi.org/10.1007/979-8-8688-1303-0_3

A Day in the Life of an Effective Developer

The door opens, and Betty enters her apartment. She's just finished her morning walk and plans on making breakfast before starting her workday. Betty opens her laptop before heading to the kitchen and checks the team schedule. Then she looks at Slack, viewing the channels with notifications meant for her. Even though multiple software changes were pushed to production while she was offline, none caused a major issue.

Finally, she notes that the morning scrum has been pushed back by 15 minutes to accommodate someone's dentist appointment. Everyone has accepted the change so that the shift won't affect the meeting.

Betty continues her morning, finishes breakfast, and logs into the morning scrum. The meeting was brief but was worth the time. During the meeting, they uncovered a potential overlap between Betty and another developer. Betty decides her work can wait while the other developer completes their task.

She opens the project management tool and assigns herself the next task on the backlog. The task is clearly defined, providing details, acceptance criteria, and images of the desired user interface (UI). She has a couple of questions but nothing blocking. Betty creates a comment, and the appropriate team member is notified. They might not respond until morning, but that's ok. She has enough to get started.

She continues with her work, receiving notifications throughout the day about issues that need her attention. These include system monitoring, async communication on several platforms, and direct communication via Slack. Betty finishes her task, creates a pull request, and takes a break before going on to her next task. Before signing off, she checks Slack and sets her status to away to let people know she can't be reached.

Betty's team is an example of what a typical day in the life of a remote developer should look like. While communication is primarily asynchronous, they have put in the effort to ensure the work from one person does not block the other. Notifications have been set up correctly to avoid unnecessary interruptions and ensure essential communications are not lost. This leads to a team that runs like it's on autopilot. Work goes into the pipeline, and a finished product is produced. For a manager, this is the best possible outcome we could hope for.

Next, let's examine some traits that all effective remote teams have in common.

Defined Roles and Responsibilities

There is no shortage of things to do when building software. Everything from configuring the servers to writing code to designing user interfaces takes time. Each requires a specific skill set to do well. Teams often have people who specialize in a specific type of work, like front-end development or user experience (UX) design.

An effective remote team has clearly defined roles and responsibilities. Each person understands what they need to work on.

Knowing What to Do Each Day

A smoothly run remote team ensures their developers start each day knowing the following.

- Who is on their team

- What project they are working on

- Where to find their next task

- When their task is expected to be finished

They have brief meetings to set high-level goals and then work from a list of well-defined tasks. Any work that needs to be completed by a specific team member is called out, and any conflicts are resolved. If a developer is blocked, they can ask questions and connect with the appropriate people. Finally, finding a new task is easy when a task is complete.

When developers understand what they are responsible for, the results are reflected in your daily scrums. They finish tasks close to the original estimates. Blockers are mostly limited to problems out of their control rather than poor planning.

Career Ladder

Effective remote teams invest in their employees' growth, which develops existing talent, boosts employee satisfaction, and provides mentorship opportunities from within the organization. Publishing career ladders outlines a clear path from one level to the next, which means that managers can work with employees to develop an individualized growth plan, which may include multiple paths for promotion. It gives employees more control over their own growth.

In addition to having a career ladder, it's always beneficial to provide training opportunities to employees. This could involve sharing resources, providing time off to attend seminars or conferences, or providing a professional development budget.

Proactive Problem-Solving

Remote teams that adopt a proactive problem-solving approach anticipate issues before they happen, which greatly reduces the number of escalated issues that pull them away from their day-to-day work. This can be demonstrated by a team's ability to control situations vs. simply reacting to problems, and it can be applied to several different areas of software development.

Let's consider a remote team working for a regional bank. They build and maintain the systems for the bank's customers, so the system must always be up and running to accept deposits and withdrawals.

The team works during normal business hours, with some developers starting work a few hours earlier or later than their co-workers. Because this team knows that uptime is critical, they have created a monitoring and alerting system informing them of unusual traffic spikes and system performance. These alerts have multiple tiers: info, warning, and critical.

One night, an alert notifies the team of a 20% spike in deposits. The developer assigned to on-call is alerted. They go to their home office and sign on. From there, they review the alert and see the uptick in traffic. The on-call documentation available on their internal wiki instructs them to spin up additional servers in preparation for the possibility of more traffic. The developer runs the provided command, and the additional server is added. They sign off for the night.

The monitoring system sends an email report of nightly user traffic in the morning to the team. The spike in deposits continued throughout the night. Since the developer on call increased capacity, the system handled the deposits without issue.

As you can see from this example, the team's forethought and planning prevented a system outage. Procedures were already in place for the on-call developer, eliminating the need to contact anyone else. This is precisely how a proactive problem-solving mindset prevents issues from happening.

Now, explore some characteristics of proactive problem-solving and how they can be applied to software development.

Anticipate Common Problems

Not all bugs are preventable. A proactive team understands this and takes the time to identify potential issues, create solutions, and provide safety nets to ensure that problems don't quickly escalate into major incidents.

Since remote teams prioritize asynchronous communication, proactive monitoring of site reliability is vital. You can't always expect everyone to be online to address issues. Instead, available developers are notified, and actions can be taken to either handle a problem or escalate it to the proper people. The following are some of the systems that remote teams set up to gain visibility into their infrastructure.

- **Monitoring** provides insight into system operations. It includes metrics like server performance, network traffic, and requests per second.

- **Alerting** tells us when something is wrong. Alerts are received via email, Slack, or text messaging.

- An **incident management process** handles problems. It includes escalation procedures, incident rooms, and on-call scheduling.

This practice also extends to the code. A proactive team understands that software is constantly changing. Each change introduces the risk of bugs and failure. To lower the risk, they put the following practices in place.

- **Design documents**: New features go through a formal request for comments procedure to identify potential issues before coding begins.

- **Automated testing**: Catch problems caused by code changes and prevent regressions.

- **Code branching strategy**: Isolate groups of changes to a feature branch. This avoids blocking team progress.

- **Pull request reviews**: Use code peer review to spot bugs or potential problems before merging into a main branch.

This section demonstrates how a proactive team plans for problems rather than only reacting when they happen. These strategies are covered in more detail later in the book.

Improving As We Go

Every change we make to our software is a chance to improve it. This is how a proactive team approaches software development. Each feature request is an opportunity to improve the code, team workflow, or system documentation. While we can't anticipate all issues that will occur, if we iterate and improve each time we interact with our product, we can eliminate many possibilities.

Learning from our mistakes and documenting the root causes of issues is crucial to remote development teams. This could involve implementing retrospectives after major releases or introducing a root cause analysis process after incidents. The documentation from these meetings can be shared with current and future engineers to spread the knowledge and continue improving future iterations of our codebase.

Build Maintainable and Flexible Systems

The proactive team adopts various practices that keep the codebase maintainable and flexible to prevent future development from slowing down and becoming error-prone. As new engineers join the team, the codebase should be intuitive, and engineers should be able to jump in and start contributing easily. The following are some of the standard practices they use when building software.

- **Design patterns**: These are common solutions to problems. For example, the model-view-controller design pattern is a common and effective way to separate user interfaces from business logic.

- **Single responsibility principle**: Create code with a single purpose to exist and a single reason to change. Allows for code to be reusable and easily tested.

- **UI component library**: It comprises reusable pieces of the UI that can be assembled into complete interfaces without duplication.

A productive remote team uses these practices to speed up development. The team constantly builds frameworks that can be reused, which prevents many bugs. The software is also easily tested via automation, which is another safety net to prevent production bugs.

Empathy

Unless you work completely alone, you interact with other people. It could be your team members or your customers. Whatever the interaction, working with others brings up all kinds of problems. A field such as software development is very opinionated and often creates heated debates about the "right" way to solve a problem.

When these debates are carried out online instead of face-to-face, the nuances of how we talk can be lost. It is easy to forget you are talking to another person with emotions who wants to do their best, just like you.

Teams that practice empathy as a primary goal see much higher productivity than teams that are quick to react in harsh, unsympathetic ways. In a healthy remote team, each member works together toward a similar goal. Instead of lashing out at a poorly worded comment on a pull request, empathic team members may suggest a video call to clarify things.

Assume Good Intentions

Working with legacy code can be a daunting experience. Some of the code can be difficult to read and frustrating to change. Every attempt to make a change introduces bugs or breaks the code altogether.

Most developer's first reaction is to get upset and blame the author for being lazy and taking shortcuts. They do this without considering the circumstances under which the developer made the change. For all we know, the original developer could have intended to create something great, but a tight deadline or lack of expertise working with that part of the application caused them to cut corners.

For example, say a developer has been tasked to add a new page for admins to view a list of users who've logged on in the past day. It's an easy task, but the developer assigned is new and unfamiliar with the team's front-end framework.

They attempted to add the new page following patterns from the framework of their last company. This approach isn't working, and the deadline is approaching fast. It would be best to take a step back and read the documentation, but there isn't enough time. Instead, the developer hacks together something that completes the task and creates a pull request.

The senior developer assigned to the pull request takes a look. The code is different from what they expected. Instead of closing the pull request with an angry comment, they reach out to the newer developer and suggest they revisit the task using paired programming. After an hour's meeting, a new pull request is created using the available framework. In addition to using a better approach, the newer developer now understands the available tools.

In our example, the senior developer encountered code that was not optimal. However, instead of reacting with frustration, they chose to take an empathetic approach. They considered the circumstances of the newer developer and realized they didn't have the knowledge needed to create the new UI correctly.

By offering help and guidance, both developers benefited. The newer developer gained a better understanding of the tools available, and the senior developer was able to foster a more collaborative and supportive team environment.

Keep Future Developers in Mind

It's unlikely that the code you write today will remain unchanged. Product managers often want to tweak functionality, and developers may discover a better way to accomplish the same results.

An empathic remote team creates code that is mindful of future maintainers. They take the time to design the code to make it easy to change. When possible, they also create documentation describing how the system works. Future developers can use this to save time and avoid mistakes when working with the code.

By considering the other developers, whether it's a new team member or even the original author, an empathic remote team sets them up for success. This approach is far more effective than making hasty changes and leaving the next person to clean up the mess.

While this is more work for the original developer, other developers won't need to rediscover assumptions and decisions made during the original development. It only takes a little extra effort to practice empathy. The results are happier, more productive, and less frustrated developers.

Positive Team Morale

One way to spot a team practicing empathy is by looking at team morale. You can look for this during meetings and one-on-one interactions. A team with positive morale shows the following signs.

- Speaks often, asking questions and providing feedback
- Leaves video on even when optional
- Offers to share accomplishments
- Multiple people want to speak
- Smiling

This isn't a complete list, but you get the idea. A team with positive morale is engaged and isn't afraid to share opinions. A single person isn't dominating the conversation, shutting down ideas as they pop up. Instead, each team member shares ideas that spark new thoughts.

The last item on the list may seem obvious, but body language can tell us a lot. Teams with low morale seem tired all the time. They look like they can't wait for the meeting to be over. You might not even have the chance to see them since they often opt to turn off video.

In contrast, teams with high morale are more energetic and ready to talk and get on with their workday.

Transparency

When working remotely, communication with our co-workers is primarily electronic. We communicate via emails, Slack messages, and video conference calls. In some companies, you may never meet someone you work with face-to-face, which is why being as transparent as possible is important. Without it, people will work in silos and be caught off-guard by unseen issues, even if those issues have been going on for some time.

This section discusses how a highly functional remote team uses transparency to build trust and foster idea-sharing.

Make Information Public

When a team practices transparency, important conversations between two people are moved to public channels. Doing so allows other developers to follow the conversation even if they aren't actively involved. This is a great way for senior developers to share knowledge without formal meetings. Any developer offline during the conversation can read it once they log on.

Public channels also serve as a public record for decision-making. These conversations can be referenced when memories fail or the decision affects other work.

For example, say that two developers are deciding how to change the authorization system. They begin their conversation in a private channel, moving it to the public engineering channel once ideas start flowing. Another developer who is logged in joins the conversation to share some ideas after working on the authorization system for their last task. A decision is reached, and the three developers sign off.

Another team member signs on after taking a long break. Before they begin their task, they see what they missed while away. After reading the conversation, they realized the proposed solution for the new authorization system conflicts with their task. Instead of continuing, they add their discovery to the conversation, including a link to their task. They look for another task to work on.

In the example, our developers made their conversation public instead of keeping it private. It resulted in additional feedback and saved another developer from wasting time on a related task. Everyone is kept in the loop regarding important decisions.

Openly Share Issues

Creating software is a complicated process. No matter how careful you are and how much you test, things will go wrong. When they do, it's better to be transparent and share the problem publicly with the team. If the problem is widespread enough, the company should be made aware to help mitigate damage.

The sooner a team knows about a problem, the faster they can work together to fix it. Keeping problems to ourselves wastes time. If the problem is openly shared, another team member might have a fix.

Let's look at an example. A developer is tasked with updating the database schema. The change is minor, adding a single new attribute. A code change is made, a pull request is approved, and changes are deployed to production. Next, the developer checks the logs and notices something is wrong. An error involving the attribute they added keeps appearing.

When a developer shares, the response needs to be constructive. Even if they are at fault, focus is on the problem and provide helpful feedback. Otherwise, teams will become reluctant to share.

The developer doesn't know what to do. They followed proper procedures for this type of change. Instead of panicking, they inform the team of the problem. One of the developers chimes in, saying they've seen this issue before. The two join a video call, and the problem is fixed. The solution was a single server reboot.

Our example showed how openly sharing issues can lead to positive outcomes. If the developer who caused the issue hadn't spoken up, the problem would have persisted for much longer than it needed.

Constructive Feedback

When a developer completes a task or writes a design document, it's helpful to have another developer review the work. Also, at the end of a sprint, having postmortems or retrospectives provides a time for the team to reflect on what went right and what went wrong. During these reviews, transparent teams aren't afraid to provide constructive feedback. This type of feedback focuses on the problem, not the person. The result is a much better final product.

On teams where feedback isn't turned into a personal attack, team members speak up rather than remaining quiet when they have something to say. As a result, important information isn't missed during team discussions.

Summary

This chapter discussed how a strong remote team functions. Each section provides details and examples of what happens when this is achieved. The result is a team that functions on autopilot, churning out high-quality code. This book teaches you the skills and tools needed to achieve a remote team dynamic like this. The next chapter begins with all the work you need to do before writing a line of code or making the first hire.

PART II

The Setup

CHAPTER 4

Ecosystem

Technology is key in making remote teams work. Remote work wouldn't be possible without many of the tools and services available to today's developers. While high-speed internet was the catalyst for this change, it was only the beginning. Technology like cheap cloud computing, multi-person video conferences, and easy code collaboration have made working from home a matter of paying for a monthly subscription.

Our goal is to create an ecosystem that promotes asynchronous communication and removes friction, getting an idea realized as code running on production. Team interactions become part of our workflow rather than something we must remember to do.

The question is, what tools do we need, and how do we configure them? With so many options available, which are the right ones for our team? We hope to answer these questions in this chapter. We cover the services you need to achieve our goal, and with the aid of specific to-do lists, outline why you need a particular service and explain how to select from the many offerings available on the market.

Don't get too hung up on picking the "best" option. What's important is that you choose something to get started. You can always change your mind later when you have more context. Many services make it easy to migrate, so the risk of choosing the wrong one is low. Let's start with one of the oldest forms of Internet communication: email.

© Carleton DiLeo, Jennifer Reyes 2025
C. DiLeo and J. Reyes, *Effective Remote Teams*,
https://doi.org/10.1007/979-8-8688-1303-0_4

Email

```
                        ♀ TO-DO
```

- Sign up and register a domain name (if using a custom domain).

- Sign up for a service email account.

- Invite or create emails for the team.

Email is the backbone of Internet communication. It was created long before the World Wide Web and hasn't changed much since it was introduced in the 1970s. When services like Gmail, Hotmail, and Yahoo Mail launched, obtaining an email address became possible for anyone with an internet connection. Now, every website requires an email address to sign up. You'll need it to sign up for all the other services in this chapter.

The primary function we need is the ability to send and receive email, but this isn't the only thing. There are additional features we need to facilitate easy team management and communication.

The following is a list of the most important.

- **Email aliases**: This offers the ability to create email addresses that deliver emails to one or more other email addresses; for example, email received at info@company_domain.com is delivered to dev1@company_domain.com and dev2@company_domain.com.

- **Calendar**: It allows the creation of meetings and events and inviting people using their email addresses. It's also important that the invitee can accept or decline the invite.

- **Shared calendar**: This offers the ability to create shared calendars with others. We can use this to display paid time off (PTO) requests and company holidays on everyone's calendar.

- **Contact list**: It provides the ability to create a list of contacts.

- **User management**: This allows the admin account to create, update, and delete email accounts on behalf of your company.

- **Enhanced security**: It can configure multifactor authentication and other password policies.

While you might find many more options helpful, the ones we have listed are needed for this book. Most cloud-based email providers have them in some form. Take time to figure out which platform works for your budget and company size.

Here are some of the options to consider.

- DNS registrar provided email (Sometimes provided for free or very cheap)

  - GoDaddy

  - Bluehost

  - Namecheap

- Big tech email

  - Gmail

  - Microsoft Outlook

  - Yahoo Mail

- Smaller tech email

  - ProtonMail

  - Zoho Mail

If you plan to use an email address with a custom domain name, buy a domain name from a DNS registrar before signing up for your email. We recommend not using your personal email since the credentials for this email are placed in a password manager to avoid loss.

Once you've registered a domain and decided on an email service, it's time to begin. The first email to create is the service email. It is the admin account for your email provider.

Pick a name that reflects its intended purpose. For example, you can name it something like "services@company_domain.com" to signify this email is used to sign up for all your services.

Make a note of the password you provided during setup. It should be secure with numbers, alpha, and special characters. This email account is the key to our entire ecosystem. We don't want it to fall into the wrong hands. Pick a good password.

Now, you can create an email address for yourself and anyone working for the company. There are a few tasks we recommend completing after you've done that. These might seem strict, but it's easier to enforce them from the start than after your team has grown. Plus, we pick a password manager to make it easy to manage.

- **Configure password policy.** Set a minimum password length of at least eight characters, require special characters, and force reset after six months.

- **Use multifactor authentication.** Require users to set up multifactor authentication.

- **Set up a fallback email.** Configure a fallback email address for the service account. You can use the same email used to register the company's domain. Do not use an email that uses your custom domain. If you lose access to your custom domain, you risk losing access to your email.

Password Manager

♥ TO-DO

- Sign up for a password manager.

- Store service email account credentials in the password manager.

- Invite the team to the password manager.

- Create team-specific vaults.

Now that you've created a service email address, we can begin signing up for our various services. We are juggling a lot of credentials, so we are picking a password manager to manage all of them.

Password managers are essential because they promote secure practices and provide a safety net against system access loss. Instead of placing credentials in text files, we save them in a password manager accessible to the team. Important keys and passwords are not lost if someone leaves the team or a computer crashes.

We store all the credentials created in this chapter in our password manager. We strongly recommend you do the same for any other services you or anyone in your company signs up for.

There are several password management services available at the time of writing this book. You may have a favorite already. We recommend that you choose one with the following features.

- **Browser and desktop integration** to integrate with desktop and/or browser via plugin.

- **Cloud sync** to synchronize credentials to the cloud for easy sharing.

- **Create shared vaults** to create separate vaults to allow organization and restricted access to our credentials.

- **Store more than credentials** to save more than credentials. This includes access keys, secret texts, and more.

- **Use a complex password generator** to generate complex passwords for you.

- **Use two-factor authentication support** to store an one-time password (OTP) with a login.

- **Provides a command line or API** to programmatically integrate with your infrastructure. This can be an SDK, API, or command line tool.

Here are some of the password managers you should check out.

- 1Password
- Bitwarden

Choose a password manager and sign up using the service email created in the earlier section. Once finished, create the following vaults and share the vaults with the team members who need access to the credentials stored in that vault.

- Engineering
- Product
- General

Store the credentials for the following accounts in the engineering vault.

- Service email account
- DNS Registrar account
- Password manager account

If sharing some credentials, like those for your HR accounting software, won't work due to security concerns, create another vault named Owner. You can store more sensitive credentials here. Finally, create an account for all the people on your team. Have everyone perform the following actions.

- Install the desktop app and browser plugin.

- Store email account credentials in a personal vault, including MFA.

Now that we have a place to store our credentials, we can begin signing up for other services. Let's move on to real-time communication.

Real-Time Chat

 TO-DO

- Sign up for a real-time chat service.

- Store real-time chat account credentials in the password manager.

- Invite the team to real-time chat service.

- Create team-specific channels.

Sending emails provides near-instant communication, no matter where the recipient is located. Still, emails are not usually read the moment they are received. People can take hours or even days to respond. They're great for formal communication between co-workers and people outside the company but do not provide the immediacy we need for day-to-day communication.

A remote team needs a way to supplement the communication we lose by not working in an office together. Without it, we feel disconnected and find it difficult to coordinate work. This can make large projects with many moving parts nearly impossible to complete on time.

To solve this problem, let's use a real-time chat service for day-to-day communication.

During the writing of this book, Slack is one of the most widely used platforms for real-time chat. Larger companies may use Microsoft Teams if their IT department is Microsoft-based. Hobby communities use Discord to replace the function of online forums. There are also several start-ups attempting to make headway in this market.

There may even be more options available when you read this book. We recommend reviewing what is available and choosing whichever option fits your budget. The following describes the feature set.

- **Channels** allow teams to create themed chat rooms to discuss different topics.

- **Direct messages** allow one-on-one communication between team members.

- **Third-party integrations** allow other services to inject messages into channels.

- **Emojis** allow additional expression beyond text.

- **Notification configuration** specifies when to be notified of messages since not all messages are pertinent to a user.

After you've picked a real-time chat service, sign up using the service email and store the account credentials in your password manager. Then, invite all the people on your team. Some real-time chat services use an invite link to do this.

Create the following channels and invite others to join.

- **General** is a channel for the entire company to talk.

- **Engineering/Development** is a channel for the developers to talk.

- **Product/Design** is a channel for product and design to talk.

We create more channels later in the book. For now, these are enough to start. Next, let's discuss video conferencing.

Video Conferencing

💡 TO-DO

- Sign up for a video conferencing service using the service email.

- Store video conferencing account credentials in the password manager.

- Configure real-time chat integration to allow starting a video conference from the chat application if available.

- Invite the team to a video conferencing service.

Real-time chat is a valuable tool for continuous team communication, but it has limitations. Text messages can be slow and lack the emotional depth that face-to-face interactions provide, no matter how many emojis you use.

Private meeting rooms, impromptu cubicle discussions, and water cooler conversations are part of everyday work for an in-person team. As a remote team, we don't have these options. Finding a way to replicate these interactions is crucial. Video conferencing provides the closest replacement. It offers a way to see and hear our co-workers, reducing the risk of misunderstandings and enhancing team dynamics.

Video conferencing isn't a new technology. Many companies have been providing the service for decades. You probably have one you prefer. For the service to integrate into our workflow, we must pick one with the following features.

- **Private meetings** to hold private one-on-one meetings

- **Group meetings** to hold group meetings with as many people as are on your team company

- **Record meetings** to record meetings for later viewing (This is helpful when some people can't attend a meeting due to scheduling conflicts.)

- **Share screen** to share computer screens

- **Meeting invite links** to share a link to allow others to join (These links can be included in calendar events.)

- **Password** to set a password for a meeting

There are many video conferencing services, and covering them all is beyond the scope of this chapter. Zoom, Google Meet, and Microsoft Teams are some of the more popular options as of the writing of this book.

Once you decide on a video conferencing service, sign up with your service email account and invite the team members. Make sure to store the account credentials in your password manager. If you can integrate with your real-time chat, do so now.

Some video conferencing services let you start a video conference using a command in your real-time chat. Any reduction in friction when starting a video conference is always welcome.

With communication handled, let's move on to setting up a service that provides a place to store our code and collaborate with our team.

Code Storage

```
┌─────────────────────────────────────────────────────────┐
│                      ♀ TO-DO                              │
└─────────────────────────────────────────────────────────┘
```

- Sign up for a GitHub using the service email.

- Store GitHub account credentials in the password manager.

- Create an organization.

- Invite the team to the organization.

- Create a Git branch called "develop" from the Git branch called main.

- Configure safeguards for the "develop" and "main" branches.

- Configure notifications.

- Create a pull request template.

Now that we've addressed communication, we need a place to store our code and assets. Unlike other sections, in which we provided several options, we suggest you use GitHub.

GitHub is a feature-rich platform for storing, collaborating, and deploying applications. It is widely used and has all the features we need to make our remote team successful.

If you want to use or must use a different solution, the ideas in this chapter should translate to other modern systems, giving you the flexibility to choose what works best. We recommend that whatever solution you pick, the backend uses Git. Older version control systems like Subversion and CVS make it difficult to implement our workflow.

The following are some of the Git-backed services available when writing this book.

- GitHub

- Gitlab

- Bitbucket

Let's move forward with GitHub. Developers often use their GitHub account for work and hobby projects. Since we want to put the account credentials used to create the organization and repository in GitHub, we don't want to use a personal account.

Instead, let's use the service email to create a new GitHub account that will own the company's organization. This allows us to disconnect ownership from a single person. We can store these account credentials in our password manager without issue.

Perform the following steps.

1. Create a new GitHub account using the service email.

2. Create an organization for your company.

3. Invite your team to the GitHub organization.

4. Create a new repository for the main application.

Add your developers to the default team provided by GitHub. Using the default team is sufficient at this time. When your team has grown, you can leverage the ability to create multiple teams inside of GitHub.

Also, we will only create a single repository rather than attempting to predict other repositories we might eventually need. You can always make new repositories for library code that are separate from the main repository.

Clone the repository to your local machine. Git should default to the "main" branch. We will change this later in the chapter, but using the "main" branch is fine for now.

Skeleton Application

Early in the book, we said we wouldn't write any code until we were all set up. However, we need to make an exception to allow us to test certain services like our hosting service. We need a bare-bones application built using your chosen programming language and framework. This skeleton web application serves as a single placeholder page.

For example, if you use Ruby on Rails, you create a new application using the Rails generators. When running the generated application on a developer machine, you would see the "Yay! You're on Rails!" page when navigating to "http://localhost:3000".

We'll leave the details to you, but your skeleton application should have the following.

- A web page that is viewable using a browser
- A passing test suite, even if that suite one has a single test
- A tool or process to deploy a web server

Commit and push the skeleton application to GitHub. Note the steps needed to set up and run the application on your local machine. You will need to document this in a later section.

Dual Branches

Create a new branch from the "main" called "develop" and push that to GitHub. The "develop" branch is the branch that your team will work from. They will create branches off this branch to build new features.

When it's time to release to production, you will create a release branch from "develop" and merge it into the "main" branch. Don't worry too much about the details at this point. We describe our Git branching strategy in later chapters.

Repository Safeguards

We want to implement several guardrails on GitHub to prevent common mistakes during development. We do this not because we don't trust our developers. People make mistakes. Because we work remotely, who those mistakes affect won't be immediately apparent. The last thing we want is to unknowingly break something, sign off for the night, and find out the next day that we ruined another developer's productivity.

We place these safeguards. Having them hardwired into our tool ensures we can't mess up. Many of these safeguards can be configured at the organizational level so that new repositories automatically receive the settings.

The following are the recommended configurations.

- **Change the default branch to develop.** When a developer clones the repo, Git sets their initial branch to "develop" instead of "main". This prevents accidental pushing to the "main" branch, which should be avoided.

- **Configure the ruleset for the "develop" and "main" branches.**

  - **Restrict deletions.** We don't want anyone accidentally deleting these branches.

  - **Require a pull request before merging.** It prevents pushing directly to branches and enforces a review process. This prevents the accidental merging of unreviewed changes.

    - Require at least one approval to merge a pull request (You can choose to implement this rule later if you are a team of 1)

- **Require status checks to pass or require workflows to pass before merging.** Require pull requests to pass a series of checks like tests or static code analysis. Making these checks automatic helps prevent mistakes. (We will configure these later.)

- **Block force pushes.** Prevent accidental force push that can cause problems for other developers. Force pushes can overwrite history and cause other developers to lose work.

- **Configure repository labels.** Labels provide visual cues to the viewer. Review the default labels and change the wording and/or color to your liking.

GitHub has a wealth of customization options. We won't cover all of them here, but it's recommended that you look through them to see if there is anything else you want to change.

Generally, configuring GitHub to be more restrictive prevents issues. While this can hinder small teams, having these restrictions prevents accidents. Less accidents means less time your team spends untangling conflicts and cleaning up messes.

As your team becomes more comfortable working within the safeguards, you can review them and disable any that seem unnecessary.

Notifications

GitHub provides many features to help facilitate communication within the platform. These options are helpful for keeping records of changes and discussing those changes. The more dialog stays in GitHub, the less time future developers will spend tracking down relevant information during troubleshooting.

One issue with keeping communication within GitHub is it can be hard to keep track of all the conversations happening at a given time. Messages can be lost in the shuffle of a busy workday. This is especially true for remote teams that work different hours.

Notifications help our team stay on top of tasks and ensure no discussion thread is abandoned. There are two ways we will deliver notifications: real-time chat and email. For email, we need to configure GitHub to notify us of the following events.

- A developer assigned as a pull requests reviewer

- Updates on the developers' open pull requests

- Updates on the developers' assigned pull requests

- Updates to watched repositories

GitHub comes with default notification settings that cover most of the actions you need to be notified about. However, you should review the settings to ensure they match what we want. GitHub may have changed what's available since we wrote this book.

Next, let's look at notifications sent to our real-time chat. At a minimum, we recommend configuring GitHub to notify your team about the creation of new pull requests. You can send these to the engineering channel or a dedicated channel if that becomes too noisy.

Notifications inform the team of new code being added to the application. Even if team members aren't directly involved with the changes, it's helpful to be kept in the loop. You may want to turn this notification off as the team grows to avoid too much noise.

The last thing we must do is create a GitHub pull request template. A template automatically fills in the description field of a new pull request with the text we define. We use this to inform the developer opening a pull request what information they are expected to provide. This is helpful since the developer doesn't have to refer to outside documentation. What is expected is placed front and center and is thus difficult to forget or ignore.

The following is an example of a pull request template.

```
Provide a description of the change. If this is a bug fix,
provide the steps to replicate the bug.

Todo:
[ ] Additional documentation
[ ] Additional Specs
[ ] Change version number

[Insert relevant screenshots]

Links: [Add relevant links]
Task: [Add link to task]
```

That should be enough configuration to move on to the next section, where we set up our project management service.

Project Management

♀ TO-DO

- Sign up for a project management tool using the service email.

- Store project management tool account credentials in the password manager.

- Create a new project.

- Configure labels.

- Configure lanes.

Over the past few years, project management tools have flooded the market. Each new offering brought its unique approach to project management and planning. They all have their strengths and weaknesses, but most people working in software development have their favorite. If you have a favorite, use it, make it work for your remote team, and skip ahead to "Create a new project." If you are interested in switching or aren't sure which platform to use, read on.

With many options available, choosing a project management tool can be overwhelming. However, the key lies in understanding your team's needs. For most teams starting out, a simple tool is more than sufficient. At this point in development, you don't need to worry as much about long-term planning or multi-team project management. You are focused on creating a minimal viable product (MVP). You need a tool to create tasks, assign them to a developer, and track progress. Simplicity is key.

As your application matures, the team's needs will change. You can move to a new service if you outgrow your project management tool. Moving to a different platform isn't as difficult as you might think. Your team has to learn a new interface, and some work is required to move the existing backlog to the new platform. Overall, the process is low effort.

Let's move on and cover the options available to you. There are two tiers of project management tools.

- **Basic**: Provides the equivalent of a whiteboard with sticky notes placed in different lanes, such as backlog, in progress, and complete. This level of tool should let you customize your lanes, manage individual tasks, and assign tasks to developers. Labels and integration with GitHub are also common.

  - Trello

  - Notion

  - Basecamp

- **Advance**: This level of tool provides much deeper customization and planning. Managers can perform resource planning, create roadmaps, switch between multiple projects, define task dependencies, generate reports on team velocity and other metrics, and configure additional integration for third-party services. The following are some of the products available when writing this book.

  - Asana

  - Jira

  - Linear

As tempting as it might be to jump straight into advanced project management, we recommend starting with a basic tool and upgrading once you've outgrown it. That way, your team can spend less time learning how to use the project management tool and more time developing features. This also gives you time to understand how your team works. Once you do, picking a new project management tool becomes easier.

After you've decided on a project management tool, do the following.

1. Sign up using the service email.

2. Store the credentials in your password manager.

3. Invite your team to the platform.

Now, we are ready to create a container to store our tasks.

Organize Your Tasks

Many of the project management tools allow you to manage an Agile workflow. The way they go about doing that is different. Each container has its own thermology for the place in which we place work. Trello has workspaces, Jira uses boards, and Linear has Teams and projects. They all boil down to a container where tasks are placed, teams are assigned to that work, and developers pull tasks. All the project management tools we've listed allow multiple containers, but we only need one at this point. As the team grows, organizing tasks into separate containers becomes necessary. Having a container per team separates work to avoid confusion.

If your project management tool supports labels, now is a good time to customize them. Don't worry too much about the names and colors of your labels. You can always change these after discussing it with your team. The following are label suggestions labels to get you started. Feel free to change them as you see fit.

- **Blocking (yellow)**: This task is blocking another.

- **Blocked (red)**: This task is being blocked.

- **In Progress (green)**: This task is actively being worked on.

- **Testing (orange)**: This task needs or is being tested.

Next, let's create lanes to organize our tasks. Lanes provide a visual way to comprehend the state of all work performed by your team. They make it easy for managers and developers to quickly understand who is working on what and at what point of the process the work is in. Gaining visibility insights by glancing at a task board is vital for remote development. We don't have the luxury of walking through an office and gathering updates from the developers. We need another way. Our task board, with its lanes, provides that substitute. It allows anyone on the team to quickly determine their status without interrupting them on real-time chat. We keep the deep concentration that remote work fosters while maintaining visibility. Figure 4-1 is an example of what lanes look like.

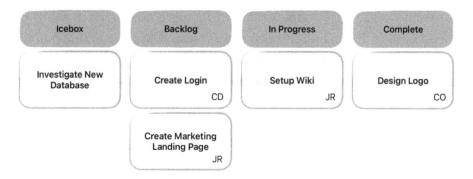

Figure 4-1. *Backlog example*

Create lanes in your project management tool that match the following.

- **Icebox**: Work that is still being planned. The tasks in this lane may need more definition or haven't been prioritized yet.

- **Backlog**: Tasks that have been reviewed and ready to be taken by a developer.

- **In Progress**: Tasks currently being worked on.

- **In Review**: Tasks being reviewed by other developers or the original requestor.

- **Complete**: Tasks that are completed and released to production.

These lanes will most likely change as your team gets comfortable working together. Your team structure also dictates which lanes you need. Teams working on mission-critical systems may have more lanes dedicated to testing and acceptance.

If the project management tool allows for GitHub integration, configure that now. When a pull request is created, we want a link between the task and the pull request. Providing this level of connectivity is helpful during pull request reviews and when trying to debug problems.

Finally, we need to configure GitHub to post notifications on the Product Slack channel when a new task is created. This allows the product team to know when new tasks are created, even when they are offline. If this becomes too noisy, create a separate channel called *product notifications*.

Hosting

🔆 TO-DO

- Sign up for a hosting provider using the service email.

- Store hosting account credentials in the password manager.

- Create a development and production environment.

- Configure alarms for abnormal behavior.

Before the launch of Amazon Web Services (AWS) and other services like Heroku, hosting a web application meant buying physical servers and installing them somewhere with a strong internet connection. Scalability, high availability, and reliability required a full-time IT staff. This came with a significant upfront cost and constant maintenance. The infrastructure team also needed to be located near the servers if something went wrong. Late-night visits to server colocations to reboot a server were not uncommon.

Cloud services have revolutionized the hosting landscape, significantly reducing the workload and costs associated with getting your application to your customers. We explore two types of cloud hosting, allowing you to choose the one that best suits your team's experience and resources.

The two hosting options are as follows.

- **Platform as a service (PaaS)**: It is easy to set up and manage, removing almost all the complexity of running a web server. It requires little knowledge to configure and maintain, but it can be pricey.

  - Heroku

  - Render

  - Koyeb

  - Fly.io

- **Cloud services provider**: It provides a lot more control over your system. Setting it up and managing it requires knowledge of networking and operating systems. This option is much cheaper, but you need someone on the team who spends a significant amount of their time managing it.

  - AWS

  - Microsoft Azure

  - Google Cloud

We recommend starting with PaaS due to the ease of setup and low overhead. During the start of development, application architecture tends to be simple. We want to move quickly, and not having to worry about managing the complex offerings of AWS saves time.

As your needs grow, you can move to a cloud service provider. We recommend you do this once the bill for your PaaS becomes too much for the company to handle or equal to or more than what you would pay a full-time DevOps person.

While Heroku was once the go-to PaaS, many new options have become available. Consider the following features.

- **Multiple environments** for the creation of environments like development, staging, production, and so forth

- **Automatic deploys** of code to servers when merging with the specified branch (This feature should allow you to configure auto deployments only when the status checks are successful.)

- **Database as a service** to set up database technology with minimal effort (This includes the ability for automated backups.)

- **Custom domain names**

- **SSL support** to configure SSL for all HTTP communication

- **Other technology support** for any other technology you need to run your web application

If you have the skills and time to set up and configure a cloud service provider, you can do so instead of signing up for PaaS. If you choose to do this now, we recommend performing the setup using tools like Terraform or Palumi for cloud service configuration and Ansible for server-specific setup. The setup takes longer but is easier to maintain since your entire system architecture is documented in code and can be rebuilt using a handful of commands.

Sign up using the service email account once you've picked your hosting service. Remember to store the credentials in your password manager.

Multiple Environments

We need to configure our service so developers can test their code and customers can access our application. The steps to set up a secure, scalable website depend on your technology stack and your company's needs. Providing that detail is beyond the scope of this book. Instead, we focus on what you need to follow our workflow.

We need two separate environments at a minimum. The following describes these environments.

- **Development**: Developers use this to test new features. This environment reflects what is currently in the "develop" GitHub branch. It's okay for this server to be broken by deploys, but it should be fixed as soon as possible.

- **Production**: Customers use this environment, which reflects the "main" GitHub branch and should be stable and not broken.

Our development environment plays a crucial role in our workflow. It allows our team to catch code issues early before they can cause significant problems in production. An immediate fix is required when code changes break in the development environment. Fixing the problem when it happens requires much less effort, as the changes are fresh in the developer's mind. Since the break is so visible, it won't go undetected and block other developers.

Eventually, you want to create a staging environment that closely mirrors production. This includes test keys for third-party integrations and running background services that process asynchronous work. The staging environment is a testing ground for release branches before merging them into the "main" branch and deploying them to production. It can also be used for load testing and testing experimental ideas. While useful, staging is unnecessary when starting a new project, but we recommend it if you have the time and funds.

Alarms

Next, we need to configure monitoring and alerting in our production environments. Monitoring and alerting provide vital insight into the system's health and performance. If something goes wrong, alarms let us know by alerting us. For example, if the application is inaccessible or the web server's CPU is higher than usual, an alarm will trigger, and we get an email and a real-time chat message.

Depending on your hosting provider, your options may be limited. If you cannot configure the following items, look to the observability platform section for other options. If your hosting does provide monitoring and alerting, configure the following items. Focus on vital systems, like your web server and database server, and then move to less critical systems. If you are having trouble determining which system to monitor, ask yourself, *If this system was unavailable, would my application crash?* If the answer is yes, add it to the following list.

- Root URL returns 200 status code or a list of important URLs

  - Web server

  - High CPU utilization

  - Low available memory

  - Low free disk space (if applicable)

  - High network traffic

- Database

  - High CPU utilization

  - Low available memory

  - Low free disk space (if applicable)

  - High network traffic

We recommend sending the alerts to an email alias your team is subscribed to and a real-time chat channel. Talk with your team about which communication method is most effective.

Observability Platform

♥ TO-DO

- If needed, sign up for an observability platform.
- Store credentials in a password manager.

Beyond simple monitoring and alerting, observability platforms are robust services that integrate with our application and hosting provider. They provide detailed insight into our system, offering useful information for your team during troubleshooting and planning. These features include the following.

- Reporting errors
- Application performance
- Database performance
- Browser performance
- Alerting

Without them, we can only guess what is going on using external factors like page load speeds. That said, you won't need to sign up for one until your application is public and people use it. If you can afford or find a free tier for a service, we recommend signing up now.

Here are some of the popular services currently available.

- Datadog

- New Relic

- Airbrake

There are so many options on the market that listing them here would be a bit much. Find one that fits your budget and supports your programming language. If you decide to skip this step, save it for later and make a note to return it once you have a public product.

Continuous Integration

♥ TO-DO

- Sign up for a continuous integration (CI) platform using the service email.

- If different from GitHub, store credentials in the password manager.

- Configure GitHub to use CI to perform checks that block pull request merges unless passing.

Every change we make to our application is a chance to introduce a bug. These bugs may be harmless or cause the production to fail. Since we are developing for the web, our users expect 24/7 access to our site. Downtime is not acceptable when people depend on our application. New features and bug fixes are released often to keep up with the demands. It's common for web development teams to release new code multiple times per day. If frequently deploying increases the risk of failure, how can we mitigate risk and prevent downtime?

Continuous integration is the answer. It's an automated process that continuously runs new code against a series of checks, including tests, security scans, and other static code analyses. Its primary role is ensuring the code we release is thoroughly vetted and bug-free. If the newly merged code doesn't meet our production standards, CI fails and notifies the team, preventing the deployment of potentially faulty code.

CI is a critical part of our development process. We integrate CI into GitHub as status checks on every pull request. These checks prevent merging into the "develop" and "main" GitHub branches until all checks pass. This ensures that our code quality is always maintained. Our hosting provider should also deny deployment if CI checks fail, further ensuring that the code our users use is bug-free.

Here are the features we need our CI platform to have.

- **Run a test suite.** We need our solution to run our test suite, at minimum. Depending on your tests, you may need the ability to interact with services like a database or third-party API.

- **Perform a static code analysis.** We need the ability to run tools to check for security vulnerabilities and syntax violations.

- **Block GitHub pull request merge.** GitHub requires your CI platform to send specific messages to signal failure.

- **Block deployment.** Your hosting solution must know if status checks failed to prevent deployment. This might be done through GitHub status checks or direct communication with the CI platform.

There are several CI platforms on the market. You can even host your own CI server using Jenkins, though this requires a lot of maintenance and knowledge. Here are some of the options available.

- GitHub workflows

- TravisCI

- CircleCI

- Codeship

GitHub workflows are one of the easiest to get started with. It supports many languages and has the features we need. It also prevents us from having to sign up and manage another service. That said, pick an option that fits your budget, team, and preferences.

If you don't plan on using GitHub workflows, sign up for a service using our service email and store the credentials in our password manager. Then, you create a GitHub workflow file or configure your CI service to perform the following checks on every GitHub pull request. The options available to you depend on your language and framework. The following checks are some we recommend.

- **Pass Test Suite (required).** All tests must pass before being deployed to production or development.

- **Pass Static Syntax Analysis (required).** Some languages have an agreed-upon style that many developers follow. Tools are available to ensure we adhere to that style. Many allow you to customize the specific rules you wish to follow. This can save time on pull request reviews since syntax irregularities are pointed out automatically. Find settings your team can work with and enforce them.

  - Ruby: Rubocop or Standardrb

- Python: Prospector or Pylint or pycodestyle

- C#: Meziantou.Analyzer

- JavaScript: JSlint and ESlint

- PHP: Phan

- **Pass Security Analysis (required if available).** This isn't always available for free or cheap, but if it is, you should add it to your status checks. It won't catch everything and isn't a replacement for peer review. It is one more way to prevent mistakes.

  - Ruby: Brakeman

  - Python: Bandit

  - C#: Meziantou.Analyzer

  - PHP: Enlightn (Laravel), Cake Fuzzer (Cake), or Parse

- **Pass Speed Analysis (optional).** These are helpful tools for catching code written in a non-performant manner. These tools may provide false positives but often are useful in catching mistakes.

  - Ruby: Fasterer

Determine the status checks you want to implement. Configure GitHub to run them using GitHub Workflows. Depending on the importance of the status check, configure it to block the merging of a pull request if failing. Also, don't forget to configure your hosting provider to block deployment to development and production when critical status checks fail.

Deployment

```
┌─────────────────────────────────────────────────────┐
│                    ♀ TO-DO                            │
└─────────────────────────────────────────────────────┘
```

- If applicable, sign up for a deployment service using our service email.

- If applicable, store deployment service credentials in the password manager.

- Configure deployment service to deploy to the development environment when merge occurs on the "develop" GitHub branch.

- Configure deployment service to deploy to the production environment when merge occurs on the "main" GitHub branch.

If you use PaaS for hosting, that service handles deployment. If you've decided to start with a cloud services provider like AWS, you must choose a service that deploys your code to all environments.

To allow our remote team to operate smoothly, deploying to the development environment should be automatic when a pull request is merged to the "develop" branch. Deploying to production can be automatic or manual when a pull request is merged to the "main" branch, depending on your comfort level. Making all deployments automatic is preferred since it means spending less time managing them and fewer mistakes.

If you need a manual deployment, for whatever reason, simplicity is key. It should be performed with a single command or a series of well-documented, straightforward steps. The more information you provide, the better. If you can automate portions with scripts, do so.

The following are some of the available options.

- GitHub workflows

- Codeship

- CircleCI

As was the case for using GitHub Workflows for CI, GitHub Workflows is an easy option for deploying to a cloud service provider. If you don't want to or can't use GitHub Workflows, you need a separate continuous deployment service to get your code to your hosting provider.

Whatever option you pick, you need to configure it to perform the following.

- Deploy to the production environment on merge to the "main" branch after all status checks pass. This step can be a manual process if you aren't ready for automatic deploys to production.

- Deploy to the development environment on merge to the "develop" branch after all status checks pass. This should be automatic.

The status checks and pull request review process ensure our code is spot-checked before deploying. If you doubt a production push is safe, you should review your GitHub configuration for pull requests, status checks, and test suite coverage. These items provide the confidence that when passing, a production deployment is a low risk. If you don't feel this way, your checks aren't thorough or strict enough. While unexpected problems always occur, your confidence in your deployment process should be high. Anything less means hesitation and second-guessing, which slows development and causes mistakes. Build a deployment process you trust; it goes a long way to improve development speed.

Let's move on to the final aspect of our ecosystem. The next section considers where to put all the knowledge we accumulate and don't want to lose.

Company Knowledge Base

♀ TO-DO

- Sign up for a wiki/knowledge base service using the service email.

- If applicable, store credentials in the password manager.

- Create baseline documentation.

The last item we need to set up is a loading area for all the essential information generated during development. Documenting our processes, system architecture, and procedures is critical in helping new developers get up to speed and support our team. It helps prevent knowledge loss from people leaving or memories fading over time. It also allows developers to work effectively without waiting for or burdening other developers. This resource should be the first place a developer looks to when they have questions.

Let's start with the entry point. The GitHub ReadMe for each repository provides an obvious place to start. Team members will visit this page multiple times per week, making it a perfect starting point.

Your ReadMe should have the following sections.

- Basic information

  - What code does the repository contain?

  - Where is the application hosted?

  - Any additional information to help the developer understand the repository at a glance

- Developer setup

  - Tools and libraries to install

- Configuration files to change

- Commands to run

- Scripts to run

- Procedures for contributing to the repo

- If this is the main repo, how to start the web app and what URL to visit

- Links to additional knowledge base pages or external links

Instead of setting up a knowledge base or creating wiki pages, you can put all the information in the GitHub Readme. Only using a ReadMe for documentation is fine for new projects since there isn't much knowledge to share.

Once the project grows, placing information in additional locations is helpful for the organization. A large ReadMe can be challenging to navigate. Breaking it into smaller chunks and using the ReadMe as an overview with links to additional pages is much easier for someone to follow.

There are several options available to host your company's knowledge base. Here are some options.

- GitHub wiki

- Slab

- Confluence

- Notion

Your choice depends on how much control you need over the editorial process. The GitHub wiki is bare-bones. It allows you to create pages using markdown and has basic search features. Other more full-featured services like Notion can be helpful for collaboration but aren't necessary for small teams.

Use the ReadMe or the GitHub wiki, or sign up for an external service. Use the service email and save the credentials in our password manager. We provide ideas for pages in the next chapter. As a rule, any information that helps developers do their jobs should be documented. All of it helps our team to be self-sufficient. Cutting down on the number of times a developer reaches out to you or another team member for help means more time for other important tasks. Being self-sufficient also means less blocked work when work hours don't align.

Your team will need to revisit these documents occasionally to update them and add additional information. When anyone on your team develops a new complex system or finds themselves always running a set of commands, write it down. Your future selves will be glad you did.

Summary

We covered a lot in this chapter. Hiring and setting up your team takes time, but it's worth the effort. All these systems offer a much smoother experience when bringing people on. You can focus on supporting your team and planning for the future.

The onboarding process and its vital role in building an effective remote team is explored in the next chapter.

CHAPTER 5

Onboarding

Adding new people to your team requires preparation and planning. When you take the time to prepare, you increase the chances of a new hire integrating successfully into the team. The first day at a new company is exciting and confusing. The new team members will have many questions that need to be answered before they can be productive.

What software do they need to install? How do they get their first task? Failing to get answers quickly means they're stuck and unable to make any progress. To prevent this, we need a frictionless onboarding process that allows the new person to start contributing as soon as possible.

Being remote, unfortunately, makes things a little more challenging. When working in an office, we can make do with a less rigid process. For example, on a person's first day at an in-person job, they would go to a given address, usually an office building. A receptionist or a team member can greet the new hire at the door and show them to their desk. From there, a member of the team can be found to start the process of getting the new person set up. Since the team is in the same office building, coordination is easy.

On a remote team, the process is a bit more chaotic. Without a detailed onboarding process, the new hire will receive a company laptop and have no idea what to do next. It could be hours before anyone on the team notices their pleas for help.

What does an onboarding process look like? This chapter explores the different aspects of onboarding, such as setting up new accounts and sending welcome emails. We cover the necessary meetings that connect new hires with the team and discuss the documentation that lets anyone new to the team work independently.

Setup

The software engineering team often acts as a new company's technical catchall. Even though writing software and managing infrastructure requires very different skills, these responsibilities fall to the developers until an infrastructure team can be hired. Setting up and configuring a new hire's services falls to you or someone on your team. In Chapter 4, we covered several services required for remote team operations. When a new person is hired, we must create accounts for them and set proper permissions.

Services

Let's start configuring the services needed to get the new hire up and running. The following are the services you need to set up before sending that initial email welcoming the new person to the team. The specific steps to complete these actions depend on the services you picked and how you decided to configure them.

- Create an email account.

- Configure access to the company's calendar.

- Configure access to the company's cloud drive.

- Create a password manager account.

  - Configure access to the vaults.

- Create a real-time chat account.

  - Add a team/group.

  - Set permissions.

  - Invite to channels.

- Create an account for a project management tool.

  - Add to team/group.

  - Configure permissions.

- Create an account for a video conferencing service.

- Create an account for a hosting platform.

  - Issue access keys.

  - Configure permissions.

- Create an account for continuous integration/ deployment service.

- Create an account for a knowledge base.

  - Configure permissions.

If you picked an email service like Gmail, it's possible to use single sign-on (SSO) to authenticate to the services that support it. This can greatly simplify the setup and deactivation of employee access.

Welcome Emails

Now that you've set up all the required services, you must send a welcome email detailing how to get access. Start by sending them the following to their personal email.

- Welcome message

- Start date

- Start time

- Login credentials for the laptop

- Instructions to login to work email account

- Instructions to email their GitHub handle (This can be their personal handle or a new one they created for work.)

- Your contact information (email, phone) and times you are available

Once you've sent this email, we need to create another email to send to the new hire's work email. This email provides information the new hire will use to navigate their first week. It includes the following.

- Zoom invite link to welcome meeting

- Link to work calendar

- Links to finalize setups for all the services configured in the last section (if not possible, credentials for the services with instructions to reset all passwords immediately)

- List of meetings to attend (add these to the calendar)

- Link to machine setup documentation

Send it now so that the email is waiting for them in their work inbox on their first day. This gives the new hire direction regardless of when they report to work. The detailed instructions for setting up their machine are in the documentation service. More on this later in the chapter.

One note: You need to configure access to GitHub when the new hire sends you their GitHub handle. We recommend using GitHub teams to manage access rather than providing access to each repository to their individual account. This makes managing access much easier, especially when removing access.

Next, let's consider the meetings a new hire should attend to help them get to know their co-workers and understand the application.

Meetings

In their first week, the new hire has several important meetings. These meetings help them get an initial understanding of your application and allow them to connect with the team. You schedule some of these meetings by sending invites via a cloud calendar service. Other meetings are scheduled by the new hire on their first day. Not skipping any of these meetings is important since they provide the vital context needed to start contributing.

This section provides sample meeting agendas, who to invite, and what to expect. The first meeting is where you, the manager, welcome the new person to the team.

Manager Welcome Meeting

The first day of a remote position can be almost anti-climactic. When working for an in-person team, the new hire is expected to show up at an office building and be shown a desk, the breakroom, and so forth. This meeting marks an official kickoff to a new job.

On that first day, people experience various emotions when stepping into a new position. For a remote worker, the hiring manager needs to replicate these feelings as best they can. Since we can't meet them in person, we will meet them via video.

Schedule a meeting shortly after their start time and invite yourself and the new hire. If their start time is 8 a.m., schedule the welcome meeting for 9 a.m. The hour between the start time and the meeting allows them to get comfortable. They can start their machine, read the welcome emails, and look at the documentation described later in this chapter. That way, they are prepared and can bring any questions or issues they encounter to the meeting.

When the meeting starts, welcome them to the company and ask if any issues have come up. The first 15 minutes of the meeting can be informal. Allow time for them to get comfortable.

After the initial conversation, cover the following items.

- Company's mission statement

- The team

- The company's work philosophy

- Anything not covered in the documentation

If your company doesn't have a mission statement, talk briefly about the goals and aims of the company. Discuss why you hired them and what you hope to achieve with their skills.

Next, talk about the team members, their roles, and when they can be found online during the day and throughout the week. Talk about expectations with different parts of the job. The following are some of the items to consider.

- Requirements for being online and expectations for being available during the day

  - **Overlap hours**: What hours, if any, are they required to be online to overlap with other team members?

  - **After-hours support**: What is the expectation for support after normal business hours?

- Meeting requirements

  - **Video on or off**: Do you require video on or off during meetings?

  - **A reliable Internet connection**: Everyone attending a meeting should plan to do so with a solid Internet connection.

- **RSVP to invites**: Respond to meeting invites to let the organizer know who is attending.

- Code of conduct

  - **No insults or threats**: Be nice.

  - **Quality vs. quantity**: The team focuses on creating quality code and features.

  - **Intellectual property confidentiality**: If there are company secrets, don't openly share them with the public.

If there is anything else that isn't documented, you should discuss it now. Ideally, everything in the welcome meeting should be available for all developers to review in the form of documentation. However, this doesn't always happen. Review these additional items and assign tasks to update the documentation.

Set aside time for questions. Go over how the new hire fits into the team and the company. Provide guidance and start them on their path to productivity. If there is time, you can review the system architecture or give them a tour of the application.

After your one-on-one meeting, the next meeting is for the new hire to get to know the team.

Team Welcome Meeting

Once you've welcomed the new person, it's time to introduce them to their co-workers. Schedule an hour-long meeting with everyone on the team. If your team is large and spread across many time zones, you can limit the meeting to those in the new hire's immediate strike team. (More on this in Chapter 7.)

During this meeting, introduce the team and let each person say something about themselves and their role. If your team is comfortable with it, have each person share a personal fact.

Next, review the team's workflow. Talk about how sprints operate. Share your screen and look at the current sprint, review the backlog, and cover the roadmap. Have some team members share interesting tasks they are currently working on.

If there is extra time, open the conversation to non-work topics. We want the new hire to get an idea of team dynamics. If not everyone on the team gets to talk, that's okay. The new hire gets dedicated time with each team member during the one-on-one meetings to get to know them better.

Individual One-on-One Meetings

Getting everyone together when new team members join is the first step to integrating them into the team, but this meeting doesn't always allow everyone time to talk. Some people take a back seat during large meetings, listening rather than participating. To overcome this, have the new hire schedule one-on-one meetings with the team to allow them time to get to know each team member.

Have the new hire spend 30 minutes of one-on-one time with each team member. They are responsible for scheduling these calls. Doing so prevents you from becoming a messenger and gives them a reason to reach out on real-time chat.

You can include instructions to schedule these meetings in your welcome email, discuss them at the team welcome meeting, or both. Before the meeting starts, suggest that both people grab a drink or snack. The company can offer to pay for the drink or snack as an added perk for attending the meeting.

There isn't any agenda for these meetings. The goal is for the new hire to get to know each team member. You may suggest talking points like work experience and hobbies.

Once the new hire has met with everyone on the team, have them meet with their strike team leader or another senior developer to review the application's technical aspects.

Pair Sessions

Working on a new application can be overwhelming. Understanding everything from the big-picture system architecture to the small details of the code takes time. Getting comfortable navigating a large, complex application can take developers months.

One way to speed up the process is to schedule a time for the new hire to pair with a senior developer. The senior developer can direct the new hire and answer questions in real time rather than waiting for a response.

Schedule a one- to two-hour meeting with the new hire and a senior developer on the team. Inform the new person to have their machine set up and review the system documentation before the meeting. Have them prepare questions or problems they've encountered as well.

During the pairing session, the senior developer reviews the system architecture. Also, look at the source code and explain how everything is organized. Talk about how the different parts interact. If the code runs on multiple systems, explain which parts run where.

Finally, work on a task together—from writing the code to creating a pull request to deploying to production. Seeing the entire process gives the new hire the knowledge and confidence they need to work on a task alone.

Once all the onboarding meetings have been completed, the new hire can explore the code and continue reading the documentation, which we review in the next section.

Documentation

Documentation is the easiest way to share information and prevent knowledge loss. It doesn't take much effort to start. Upon creating a repository, a ReadMe is generated for you. Additional information that doesn't belong in the ReadMe can be placed in separate GitHub wiki pages. If you don't care for the GitHub wiki, other inexpensive services offer additional control over access and the editing process.

The key is to make it easily accessible and easy to update. Once we create a document, we must update it and add more as our application evolves. Even though you are the one to start the documentation, it's everyone's responsibility to contribute. The documentation must be updated whenever a new system is developed or a new process is added to the workflow. If you find the team is forgetting to do this, add an item to the pull request checklist as a reminder.

This section covers the documentation you need to create a successful onboarding experience. Not only does the documentation help the new hires become productive team members, but it also helps the existing team. By documenting all aspects of our application, developers working on an unfamiliar system have a resource to guide them.

We also document to prevent knowledge loss. We build our team with the hope people will stay. The reality is this isn't always what happens. People leave for one reason or another. Having them document their knowledge when it's fresh in their minds prevents it from disappearing when they leave.

Let's begin with the technical documentation that describes how everything works.

System Documentation

Becoming productive in a new codebase is not easy. The first time a developer downloads an application's source code and opens it in a text editor, everything is unknown, and there are many questions. What framework was the web application created with? What design patterns are being used? What user actions trigger asynchronous processes, and what effect do they have on our database? The list grows as the developer dives deeper, peeling back the layers and uncovering the hidden complexities.

Being familiar with the application's programming language does help with basic comprehension, but only so much. Imagine trying to read a book where the pages are out of order. You may understand the language, but making sense of the story requires you to connect several disparate paragraphs into something whole.

Parsing hundreds of code files is much the same. The challenge is not understanding a single statement; it's understanding the context in a larger picture. It takes time to assemble these parts in our heads. Documentation helps speed up this process by giving the developer context. The reader gains a leg up by providing detailed information about how everything fits together. Diagrams help visualize complex concepts and are great additions to our text.

You decide where the documents live. You can create a single document that contains everything, which is convenient since all the information is in one place, but it can be difficult for developers to parse.

You can split the content into multiple documents connected using the GitHub ReadMe. This makes finding pertinent information easier since the ReadMe acts like a table of contents for all the docs. The downside is keeping track of all these pages can be problematic. Orphaned wiki pages can be lost and only found in a list view of all pages on the wiki service.

Pick a strategy that works for you. We recommend the single-document approach until your application has grown to the point where there is too much information. Then, move the chunks to easily digestible wiki pages.

The documents you need are covered in this section. This list isn't comprehensive since there are many ways to describe how a system works. Use this section as a guide to get you started.

System Architecture

This part of the document describes the servers, services, and databases required for your web application to work. Don't leave out any parts, no matter how small a role it plays. We want to capture a high-level picture of all the different moving parts.

If your code is spread across multiple servers, highlight which parts of the application run on which servers. Provide explanations about why you picked a specific technology. Make a note of any drawbacks to your current technology stack.

Make sure to create diagrams to help with visualization. Figure 5-1 is an example of a simple web application running on two AWS EC2 servers with a load balancer in front. AWS RDS hosts the database, and AWS ElastiCache hosts the cache.

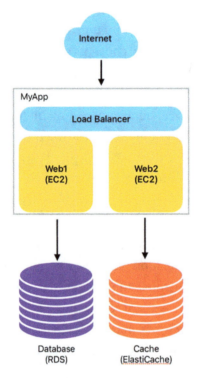

Figure 5-1. *Example of a system diagram*

Once you've captured the high-level systems, let's move on to the application specific.

Application Architecture

In this document, we describe how the parts of our application are organized together to form a whole. We also describe each part's role in the larger picture and how that part interacts with the others.

We should provide context for design decisions, such as which patterns were chosen and why. We should also give instructions for how to use and extend the code and provide plenty of code examples where applicable.

Create diagrams to visualize how the parts fit together. Figure 5-2 is an example of a simple web application that uses the model-view-controller design pattern to organize its concerns into separate parts. This diagram shows where each part sits on the stack and how our code separates a request from the database.

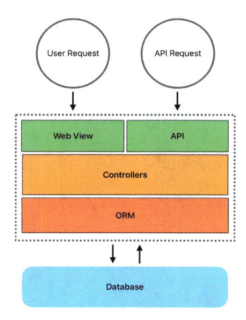

Figure 5-2. *Example of an application diagram*

Now, you have context at the high-level system and the application level. Next, let's look at how requests and data flow through our system.

Data Flow

In the previous sections, we described our high-level system and application design. By this point in our document, the reader should have a good idea of how the application is structured and have enough understanding to start looking at the code. We won't stop there, though. We also want to show how requests and data flow through our system. Think of the section before this as the static view of our application, while this section is our application in motion.

This section describes and illustrates how users interact with the application. It also shows how our automated systems manipulate data in the background and perform functions hidden from the user. Like all the previous sections, diagrams are key.

Figure 5-3 is an example of a diagram demonstrating how a user request flows through our system, triggering jobs that fetch data and send notifications via email.

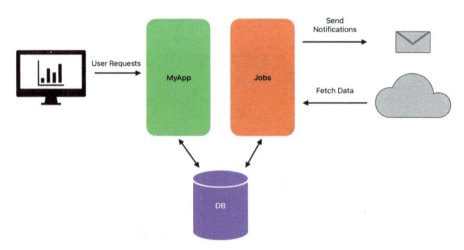

Figure 5-3. *Example of a request*

A complex application can have many of these types of requests and data flows. Limit your document to the ones that illustrate primary system functions. Once you've captured the important ones, the reader can figure out the smaller ones while looking at the code.

Let's move on to the final part of our documentation, which describes the dependencies between parts of our application.

Dependencies

As a codebase matures, common functionality is spun off into different libraries to improve organization, allow teams to work independently from one another, and ease release management. With the increased flexibility comes complexity that can make understanding how everything fits together difficult. This section helps ease that strain by describing the dependencies between the different libraries.

Create a diagram like the one in Figure 5-4. In our example, the main part of the application, MyApp, is at the top. MyApp relies on authentication and file parser libraries. Both of these libraries rely on a logging library.

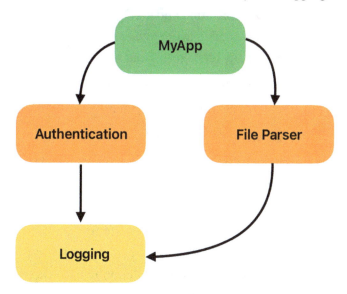

Figure 5-4. *Example of a dependency chart*

We are only showing internal libraries and not external libraries. This section is unnecessary if your application is a single monolith application with no code separation.

We've covered the basics of how the application works. Next, let's explore how to deploy our application to production.

Deployment

Regardless of how simple the application is, there is a process to deploy it to production. That process might be simple, only requiring a single button press. No matter what the process is, documenting how to deploy is important. For a new hire, step-by-step guides are key to building confidence and independence.

Create a section in your documentation that describes the process of releasing to production and staging. Be thorough and include everything, even little steps that seem obvious.

Make sure to include the following.

- **Setup**: Provide installation and configuration instructions for any software needed to deploy. Also, include instructions for any repositories that need to be cloned.

- **Commands**: Provide any commands that must be run before, during, and after a deployment.

- **Web UI**: Provide URLs, screenshots, and instructions for any web UIs that need to be used. This can include your hosting provider, your application, and any third-party services you use.

- **Configuration**: Provide instructions for updating text files, making database changes, or changing settings in a web UI. If some of these are dependent on certain conditions, define them here.

- **Testing**: Provide instructions for how to verify a
  deployment was successful. Monitoring error reporting
  services, visiting key pages, or running an automated
  script are some examples.

Providing screenshots is always helpful, but update these as UI
elements change. One nice side effect of documenting a deployment
process is that it allows you to spot ways to automate certain parts.

Now that we've provided a guide for getting code to production, let's
move on to the new hire machine setup.

Machine Setup

Getting a developer's machine set up and ready for coding can be difficult
when working remotely. Depending on how the new person receives their
machine (most likely in the mail directly from the store), they might do the
setup from scratch. Giving instructions over the phone or video conference
can be slow and frustrating. When there is no documentation, you'll rely
on memory, which can be faulty. Exact software versions and steps are
hard to recall years or even months after performing them.

As your application becomes more complex, the setup only gets worse.
Using technologies like Docker to containerize system configuration can
help, but there are always steps to get a new machine up and running.

Documenting how to configure a machine is necessary. If the
document is updated, you can send a link to a new hire instead of taking
time out of the team's day to show them. Existing team members receiving
a new machine can also refer to this guide—no guesswork needed.

One way to maintain an up-to-date guide is by having anyone who
uses it update the changes they encounter. The contents of the guide
may vary wildly depending on your technology stack. Regardless of your
application, this part of the document should have the following sections.

- Pre-requisites
    - Libraries to install (OpenSSL, GCC, etc.)
    - Tools to install (IDE, SSH client, Ansible, etc.)
    - Services to install (Postgres, Redis, Docker, etc.)
    - Configuration to perform
- Application setup
    - Clone GitHub repository
    - Commands to run
    - Configuration files and environment variables to set
    - Commands to run to seed or restore the database
    - How to start all the required services
- Verification
    - Commands to start the application
    - Commands to deploy to staging and production environments
    - Commands to run tests

Provide exact software versions, which is helpful when troubleshooting problems with new machines. Often, when configuring a brand-new machine, newer versions of libraries that are incompatible with your application get installed. Having the expected version in the documentation can provide valuable clues to help the developer troubleshoot problems themselves. Make sure to add notes of any known pitfalls or errors and how to solve them.

As your application evolves, you need to make changes to this document. If keeping the document up to date becomes a problem, add a to-do item to your pull request template to check the setup documentation when a new library is added, or a major change is made to the application.

After the new hire sets up their machine, the next step is having them make a small change to the application, create a pull request, and deploy it to production. If they can accomplish that, their machine will be set up correctly, and they will be ready to contribute. We need to add this process to either the machine setup documentation or in a separate document. Describe how to get changes from a developer machine into GitHub and finally to production. You need to cover the following items for this guide, which we call "My first commit guide."

- How to find and assign yourself a task

- How to commit code to your local Git repository

- How to push a branch to GitHub

- How to create a pull request to merge your branch into the develop branch

- How to request a pull request review

- How to handle status checks

    - How to view errors

    - How to fix errors

- When is it okay to merge a pull request

- How to deploy to a staging environment and test

- How to deploy to the production environment

Creating an initial task to assign to all new hires streamlines this part of the onboarding. An example would be for them to add a photo and description of themselves to the company's About page. This change is low-risk to production and runs them through the entire process. You can even add the task to your welcome email template.

Once new hires complete the machine setup document, they are ready to contribute to a sprint. If they have questions, they reach out to the team for help. If we were thorough, this should be a rare occurrence. Our documentation is a work in progress. It gets better the more it's used. As it improves, it becomes a valuable tool that enables our developers to find solutions independently and prevents them from waiting for help to be available.

If needed, make a separate machine setup document for the product team. A product team machine setup likely involves fewer steps and complexity than a developer's machine, but it always helps to have more documentation.

Summary

This chapter covered ways to provide a positive onboarding experience for new team members. When a new hire receives a work machine, they need to do many things to do before they can start contributing. We send welcome emails to provide a starting place, including first steps and links to documentation. They must attend several meetings to connect with the team, which provides guidance.

Finally, documentation provides education on the application internals and step-by-step guides for setting up their new machine. Hopefully, if we've done the work, they'll be ready to contribute and increase the team's velocity.

Now that the new hire is ready to work, the next chapter looks at a typical workweek.

PART III

The Work

CHAPTER 6

The Workweek

Processes are integral to software development, but not everyone enjoys them. Waiting for continuous integration (CI) to pass before deploying a hotfix to production can test our patience, especially when production is offline. It's tempting to skip steps for special situations, but this slippery slope can lead to mistakes. Sometimes, subverting our process might be necessary, but we want this to be an exception rather than a regular occurrence.

For the other 99% of the time, the process is great. It provides direction and guardrails within which the team can work. More often, it prevents unnecessary issues caused by human error. It's not hard to understand why. Imagine a team with dozens of developers working entirely independently from one another with no process. Duplicated work and conflicts would be part of everyday life, grinding progress to a halt. Developers would spend most of their time figuring out how to untangle messes. Nothing would get done.

The rigidness of your process depends on your team. Small teams will work well with a looser process, while a large team will benefit from something more rigid. Teams that have proven mindful of their work may benefit from less process.

When your team strikes the right balance between flexibility and structure, the workweek becomes predictable, and projects are more likely to finish on time. The team will celebrate more successes than setbacks, and the rest of the company will consider the application stable. Developers may start their week with a clear direction when the process is working. They can answer the following statements without hesitation.

© Carleton DiLeo, Jennifer Reyes 2025
C. DiLeo and J. Reyes, *Effective Remote Teams*,
https://doi.org/10.1007/979-8-8688-1303-0_6

- What meetings do I need to attend, and when are they scheduled?

- When do my assigned tasks need to be completed?

- When are production releases scheduled?

- Who will review my pull requests?

- What will I be working on next?

Another benefit of a defined process is that developers' concerns are narrowed, allowing them to focus on their work. They don't have to worry about wasted effort or confusion from an ad hoc approach. Everyone on the team understands their role, responsibilities on a project, and expectations for the sprint.

Consider an artist working on a painting. If they had an unlimited canvas size or no deadline, the project might feel overwhelming, and they might never complete the painting. There are too many possibilities. If, instead, they were given a canvas limitation of 8″ × 11″ and a two-week deadline, suddenly, their task would be focused. The constraints become a benefit by freeing the artist's mind to focus on the most important part of the task: painting. Software development is much the same. Our process is the constraint that lets the developer shut out the noise and focus on their code.

This chapter focuses on your team's workweek, describing a process for your sprints and how to manage day-to-day work, highlighted by goals set forth at the "prior to," "during," and "after" sprint stages. We provide a process around planning and talk about getting the completed code to production. We also explain how clearly defining roles and responsibilities is important to team success and how to build for the future.

Let's start by exploring an effective workweek in software development.

Ideal Workweek

Sheena had a relaxing weekend and returned to work refreshed. It's Monday morning, and she's at the local coffee shop, ordered a drink and settled into her favorite corner. Sheena opened her company-issued laptop and reviewed all the notifications and messages received since Friday. Her manager provided a helpful checklist of items to check each morning, which she printed and placed on the inside of her notebook.

Next, Sheena reviewed the feedback on an open pull request and made a few changes. She then pinged the reviewer over chat, who approved the pull request. All the status checks ran and passed, signaling that the request was ready, so Sheena merged it into the "develop" branch.

Her team releases to production once a week, on Monday at 1 p.m. PST. That means her work will be included in the next release. She made a note to get lunch before 1 p.m. PST so she could watch the deployment.

Later that day, after the production release, the team met on Zoom to discuss the previous sprint. Sheena has prepared notes. She discovered some issues with the review process that she wanted to share with the team.

On Tuesday, Sheena attended the sprint planning meeting. She informed the manager that a few tasks needed more definition. After reviewing the remaining tasks, Sheena was told her focus would switch from back-end to front-end development during this sprint. She would be working on Robin's team. Robin is a senior front-end developer, so it is an opportunity for Sheena to learn. She is assigned her first task, reviews it, and reads documentation for the remainder of the day to learn about the front-end framework used by the team.

The workweek continues. Each day, Sheena provides a quick update (daily scrum) via Slack in the morning. This update lets the team know what she did, what she's working on, and any blockers.

She grabs a new task from the backlog and notices a medium-sized estimate attached. She has until the end of the week to work on it. She considered using a new JavaScript library to handle one of the dropdowns, but since she's new to front-end development, she opted to use the existing library in the code.

On Thursday, she reviewed her teammates' daily scrum message and discovered John had taken a task that overlapped hers. After a quick Slack discussion, they scheduled a paired programming video call to work through the conflict later that day.

Friday arrives, and Sheena puts the finishing touches on her task. She created a pull request and assigned a reviewer. Before Sheena logs off for the weekend, she reviews all her communication and responds to a message about a feature she developed as part of the back-end team. Satisfied with her progress, she logs off and enjoys her weekend.

Agile Approach

Since its introduction in the early 2000s, the Agile Scrum methodology has changed how the web development community works. It has mostly replaced the older methodologies like waterfall, which involves planning everything upfront and completing all the work in one big uninterrupted block of time. When done, the application is released to the users.

With its shorter work cycles and flexibility, Agile quickly outshone traditional methodologies. The ability to adapt to issues as they arise, rather than waiting until the end of the project, was a game-changer. Instead of exhaustive planning, teams could start with a rough idea and refine it as they progress. As more features are completed, the more user feedback we receive, the more we learn about our project.

Agile lets us use that knowledge gained as soon as possible, as soon as the next sprint, saving us time, money, and frustration. Agile also provides tools for keeping everyone in sync. Daily updates catch conflicts early, and weekly planning lets the team take a step back and evaluate performance.

Agile's emphasis on constant communication is particularly beneficial for remote teams. Remote work's inherent isolation can lead to prolonged periods of work without team interactions. Agile's regular updates help keep everyone on the same page and prevent such isolation.

Sprints provide short-defined windows of work that require teams to check back in. If the team decides it's on the wrong path, it can correct course before it's too late.

Agile's focus on visibility keeps everyone informed and facilitates decision-making, reducing the likelihood of misunderstandings.

It's a lightweight process, so implementation requires little effort. This is why it's our methodology of choice. This book might not follow Agile scrum to the tee. If you want to follow a more rigid approach, please do so. Also, the goal of this book isn't to teach you the ins and outs of the Agile methodology. There are many great resources already available for this. Instead, we examine how Agile fits into our approach to running a remote team. Before discussing what happens during a sprint, we need to consider how to plan for one.

Before the Sprint

Before we begin a sprint, we need to plan. The effort required to prepare for a sprint varies depending on where you are in your application's lifecycle.

Early in development, planning can take several meetings to build a solid backlog. You need to iterate on ideas until they are ready. The planning meetings are shorter when your team is fully engaged in development.

A general rule is that the shorter the sprint, the shorter these planning sessions will be. One—to two-week sprints are usually the sweet spot: short enough that planning isn't a chore but long enough to allow the team time to focus. It's important to stay on top of planning. Schedule regular planning meetings. Don't wait until the backlog is empty to fill it. Doing so risks your team running out of things to do. In the worst-case scenario, your team will finish a project only to discover there is nothing to work on. Let's stay ahead of our team by building a healthy backlog of work, starting with the long-term roadmap.

Roadmap Meeting

💡 GOALS

- Brainstorm new projects.
- Review existing projects.
- Prioritize projects.

As mentioned, planning your first sprint takes much longer than planning for future sprints. When starting, it's important to strike a balance between detailed planning and maintaining momentum. This ensures progress without getting bogged down in unnecessary details.

When you haven't written any code, the possibilities are endless, and narrowing the focus to something actionable takes some time. This process could take weeks or even months, depending on the application. We don't want to dive too deep, but we need enough details to allow the team to build a solid foundation.

Many questions need to be answered during this time.

- Do the users require a login?
- Will there be an API for external developers?
- Are there different parts of the app? For example, a marketing site and a user dashboard.
- What is the expected workload (Requests per second)?

This is only a sample of the questions that need to be answered. Take your time, but don't go overboard. There will be time to finalize ideas as development is underway. This meeting aims to outline projects and determine what your team will work on in the first sprint and beyond. You'll need enough work to fill a couple of sprints. If your sprint is two weeks long, that's four to six weeks of work.

Let's consider the purpose of these meetings.

- Brainstorm new projects

- Review existing projects

    - Have priorities changed?

    - Can we provide more details?

    - Can we create tasks?

- Prioritize all projects

- Determine a rough estimate of how long each project will take

- Create rough mock-ups or system diagrams

Brainstorm some ideas and then organize them into projects. At first, projects are a nebulous concept. As you iterate, they form into concrete ideas.

When the application is new, plan wide. You are creating the application's building blocks. Solve the basic user interaction loop before polishing out the rough edges.

Also, keep your notes, mock-ups, and diagrams for whatever is discussed. You never know what will be useful in the future. It's often helpful to review older design ideas when developing new features. Once you've outlined your first couple of projects, you need to define the work that goes into realizing them.

Backlog Definition Meeting

♥ GOALS

- Create new tasks.

- Determine work for the next two sprints.

- Refine existing tasks.

Our next meeting differs from road mapping because it focuses on the near term. This meeting includes everything from the next sprint to projects two to three months out. You can combine this meeting with the road mapping meeting but avoid getting lost in discussions of projects planned too far in advance. Put the majority of the time into work for the next few weeks. Spend less time on projects as you get further out. Our goal for this meeting is to figure out what the team is working on now and set the stage for future planning.

Start the meeting by reviewing the current project.

- What tasks remain?

- Is the task prioritized correctly?

- Do any tasks need more detail?

- Are there any new tasks you should add?

- Are there any tasks you should remove?

- Are you on schedule? If not, how can you change the project to meet the deadline, or do you need to move the deadline?

Once you've answered these questions for the current project, move on to the next project. Ask the same questions, but don't go into as much detail the farther out the project is. Since we plan regularly, those projects eventually become clearer and filled in with tasks. Spending too much time on projects that won't be worked on for months could mean wasted effort when those projects change or are removed completely.

Next, let's look at creating tasks. All tasks go into your project management tool. New tasks that haven't been fully fleshed out should be placed in an Icebox or its equivalent. Tasks can be promoted to a project's backlog or equivalent as you iterate and finalize details. Tasks located in the backlog are ready for a developer to work on. Tasks at the top of the backlog are of higher priority than those at the bottom.

There are different approaches to writing a task. Agile calls them "stories" and suggests wording that describes the actor, the action, and the result. However, if you decide to write your tasks, make sure they at least have the following.

- Strong title

- Detailed description of the expected outcome

- For bugs, include the steps to reproduce the issue

- Include relevant mock-ups

- Provide links or reference materials for context

- Add color code labels

- Associated project with a project

Whether or not you add more than what we've provided is up to you. Just make sure you have these items. If your project management tool allows for templates, we recommend configuring them as a guide to what your ideal task looks like. Like pull request templates, a task template is one less thing the team must remember. It's also one less thing to review with a new hire. It's baked into our tools, so they can't miss it.

Review your tasks and order them based on priority and dependency. Once done, you can pull tasks into the next sprint backlog. Add enough work to the sprint to keep the team busy, but leave some room. Not every sprint finishes with all tasks completed, so leave space for that work.

If you can, add tasks to the next sprint as well. If there is no way to signify the tasks in the next sprint, create a task with the title "end of sprint" and place it at the end of the current sprint.

Perform a final check. Make sure dependencies are declared. Review and fix any tasks that lack detail. Add labels. Anything you can do to avoid a developer taking a task and feeling like they don't have enough information to start is welcome.

Now, we are ready for the next step: developer review.

Senior Developer Review

♥ GOALS

- Provide technical oversight.

- Create initial estimates.

- Give feedback.

Our next step in the planning process is the senior developer review. In this step, we allow our senior developers time to review the work planned for the upcoming sprint. They review each task and provide feedback and an initial estimate. The product team reviews the feedback, makes corrections, and re-prioritizes if estimates are not what was expected.

Limit the review to only your senior developers or higher. You can do the review as a meeting or assign it as an independent weekly task, but don't do it as part of your sprint planning meeting. Doing so saves your team a lot of time and effort.

Senior developers have a deeper understanding of the application and years of experience. They can quickly vet tasks for errors, determine technical viability, and even determine whether a task is needed.

The rest of the team doesn't need to be part of these early conversations. Let them focus on their work. The sprint planning meeting allows them time to challenge estimates and give feedback. When done correctly, the senior developer review makes your sprint planning meeting short and efficient. The team can meet, discuss, and be on their way to more important things.

Let's go over what the senior developer review involves. You can give the reviewer the following action items as a guide.

- Does the task make sense?

- Is there any missing context or details?

- Is the task technically possible?

- Is the task necessary?

- How long will the task take?

If the reviewer can correct any issues themselves, they should do so. If your project management tools have notifications, they should notify the person who created the task, keeping them in the loop. When possible, keep conversations in the comments section of the task.

The reviewer should spend 30 minutes to an hour reviewing the work. If more time is required, this is a sign that not enough time is being spent on planning. Estimates should be a best guess based on their experience. If there are any issues with the task, inform the product team by real-time chat, add the label "needs more definition," and move on.

The product team reviews any feedback and responds as soon as possible. If the initial estimate for the work is more than can be completed in the sprint, the product team reworks tasks to allow lower estimates or move tasks to the following sprint.

Once the back-and-forth is complete, you are ready to involve other team members.

Sprint Planning Meeting

♀ GOALS

- Review the upcoming sprint.

- Provide feedback.

- Verify estimates.

- Give everyone on the team a task.

We've done a lot of planning to get to this point, and it will be worth it when you breeze through the sprint planning meeting. You might have noticed that the further we get in the process, the more of the team we involve.

Not involving everyone at every point in the process is an intentional choice. Developers working on the micro-focused act of writing code shouldn't have to worry about the macro decisions of planning. The context switching involved can be mentally taxing and require a completely different skill set.

Imagine being a construction worker who goes from operating heavy machinery to hanging glass windows to planning the construction of a house. While all jobs are required to build a new home, they require different skills and finesse.

Building software is similar. Everyone has a role to play and different stages of the process. Requiring everyone to do everything means no one can focus enough to do anything well.

Also, not everyone has the skills to perform every function on a team. Senior developers may have the experience to be flexible, but what about junior developers? They have limited knowledge and shouldn't be expected to perform at the same level. Giving them skill-appropriate responsibilities allows them to grow with more minor successes rather than major failures.

We aren't saying that junior developers shouldn't have a say in how a task is implemented or that developers aren't entitled to push back against Product when they request the impossible. There is a time and a place. The outlined process lets the team voice their concerns about important work when right.

Now that we are on the same page, let's talk about the details of the sprint planning meeting. The following outlines an agenda you can use to guide you.

- The manager welcomes everyone and shares their screen.

- The manager opens the project management tool and navigates to the upcoming sprint.

- The manager opens each task and reads it.

- The team asks questions and makes comments about the task.

- Any tasks that aren't ready are removed from the sprint.

- Missing tasks are added.

- If the sprint has too much work, the lowest-priority tasks are moved to the next sprint.

If you've done a good job planning, this meeting should be short. Your work iterating on and polishing tasks has made them easy to understand. The senior developer review has removed technical discrepancies and provided estimates. What's left for the team is the low-hanging fruit that may have been missed.

Don't let detailed conversations make the meeting drag. Move these until after the planning meeting with only the needed people. If the task requires too much debate to include in the sprint, remove it and place it back on the Icebox for Product to revisit. If the estimate is in doubt, use methods like sprint poker to get an estimate quickly. Significant discrepancies between individual estimates should be discussed. Knowing when to punt on a task isn't an exact science. If you are sensing a lot of confusion, err on the side of caution and send it back to the drawing board.

Once you've reviewed the entire backlog, assign a task to each team member. Conclude the meeting and let the sprint begin.

The next section discusses what happens during the sprint. This includes a couple of meetings to keep the team in sync.

During the Sprint

The focus of a sprint is to complete all the work in the backlog. We are "sprinting" toward the finish line, avoiding distractions to get it all done. Once the sprint is complete, we pause, review our progress, and move on to the next sprint. This continues indefinitely; each sprint hopefully goes better than the last.

During the sprint planning, developers are assigned a task. Once they've completed that task, they take another from the top of the backlog. Like a pile, tasks are completed one by one until the backlog is empty or the sprint ends.

When a developer takes a task, have them assign it to themselves using the project management tool. As they work on the task, they move it through the different lanes, signaling the different states of progress. If something is blocking the task, mark it with a "blocked" label and provide a reason for marking it blocked in the comments. Anything a developer can do to indicate the status of a task is helpful to others when reviewing the backlog.

Information allows the team to work asynchronously. Developers in different time zones working at different hours can review the project management tool for a snapshot of the team's progress. When we are successful, it doesn't matter what time a developer is online; they are able to find the answers they need.

Next, let's discuss how to keep the team in sync with a daily meeting.

Daily Scrum/Standup Meeting

💡 GOALS

- Identify conflicts or issues.

- Keep the team in sync.

Writing code is a deeply intense process. Developers can go hours working out problems and building a solution. While this concentration is vital for building quality software, keeping in sync with our team is also important. Going for long periods without updating the team can sometimes spell disaster.

For example, imagine a developer who spends weeks creating a feature in isolation only to discover another developer has been working on a duplicate task. The other developer's work has already been released to production. Now, both developers have to spend their valuable time untangling the mess. A simple daily update can catch conflicts much earlier, avoiding wasted effort.

The standup or daily scrum requires each dev to share their work with the team at the start of their day. Standup doesn't have to be a formal meeting. Instead, it can be completed via text updates in either the engineering channel or a separate channel in your real-time chat called "Standup."

Depending on your team, you may decide to have a video call—no longer than 15 minutes—to keep the team feeling connected. If time zones prevent this, text updates are a fine alternative. Whether the team reads or listens to updates, they must review all updates for conflicts and issues with their work. Additional discussions should be performed in real-time chat or a video call outside the standup meeting.

Whether you decide to meet on video or post a text update, there are three things developers must provide.

- **What I did:** A brief list of what was done the prior workday. For example, "Created admin UI for managing users."

- **What I'm doing:** A brief list of what is to be done today; for example, in the "Documenting deploy process."

- **Blockers:** A brief list of problems blocking the progression of a task. For example, "Waiting for a review of PR #123".

Be brief, and don't provide too much detail. We want highlights, not detailed play-by-play breakdowns. Team members read or listen to the updates. Feedback can be given, but more extended conversations should happen outside this meeting or channel. You can have them out in the open on an engineering channel, or you can consider a video conference call to minimize distractions. Either way, avoid including people who don't need to be involved. Stick to quick updates and time limits. We want the team to get informed and return to work quickly.

Failing to abide by this turns our meetings into hour-long slogs where most participants tune out. Conversations are essential to software development, but they can quickly become unproductive use of time. Many issues can be resolved using a few messages over real-time chat, thus saving the team many hours that can be spent doing more meaningful work.

Next, let's explore a mid-sprint meeting focused on keeping the team synced and ensuring the successful completion of the sprint.

Weekly Sync Meeting

💡 GOALS

Allow course corrections for issues or questions that came up during sprint.

Depending on the length of your sprint, you may not need a mid-sprint update meeting. A one-week sprint, for example, does not need a mid-week meeting. Also, a weekly update may be unnecessary if your team is operating smoothly, regardless of the sprint length.

The mid-week sprint meeting occurs on Monday or Tuesday following the sprint planning meeting. During this meeting, your team discusses progress, issues, and anything related to the sprint. Some of the items that may come up are as follows.

- Tasks sent back to the product team for further development

- Important lessons learned

- Unforeseen complexity on a task

- New libraries introduced into the application

- New systems

- New features

- Incidents

You can also use this time for show-and-tell. Show-and-tell allows developers to demonstrate new features, walk through code, and share system diagrams. This is helpful for other developers who might one day work on that part of the code.

However you use the time during this meeting, the team should come prepared. Before the meeting, everyone should think of any questions, issues, or code they want to share. You can have the team send you their notes before the meeting so you can include them in the agenda. This allows other team members a chance to review and come up with additional questions.

The more prepared the team is for the meeting, the more structured it is and the easier it is to keep it within a reasonable time limit while covering everything. Remember to move deeper discussions to other meetings.

After the weekly sync meeting, continue working on the backlog. The sprint is complete when all the tasks in the backlog have been finished or time runs out. Once this happens, we move on to our retrospective review meeting.

After the Sprint

Once a sprint is completed, the next sprint begins. This development loop continues indefinitely, but before we move on, let's take some time to reflect on our progress. By stepping back and looking at what went right and what went wrong during the sprint, we can work to improve shortcomings and double down on what is working.

Our primary tool for accomplishing this is the retrospective meeting. This meeting gives the team time to air grievances and praise accomplishments.

Retrospective Meeting

💡 GOALS

- Discuss what worked.
- Discuss what went wrong.
- Create action items to correct problems.

No matter how much we plan and prepare, things may go wrong. It's a natural part of software development. Hiding our issues doesn't make them go away. Instead, we want to place them front and center for the team to discuss. Doing so gives the team a chance to reflect. We want to highlight our failures without blaming individual developers. Finding who's at fault is not the purpose of the retrospective meeting. Its purpose is to normalize talking about successes and failures. Developers want to grow and get better. The only way to do that is to acknowledge our shortcomings while praising our strengths. If we do this after each sprint, our team gradually improves and becomes better.

After the sprint, schedule a one-hour meeting with the entire team. Everyone should come prepared with one thing that went right and one thing that went wrong. Even if a developer feels there is more they want to discuss, limiting forces us to make hard choices and focus on what's most important. Don't discard the other issues. Hold onto them for the next meeting.

Start the meeting and have each developer share. Wait for questions and comments until the end. Have everyone assign importance to each item on the "what went wrong" and "what went right" list. For example, if there are ten items on a list, assign a number from 1 to 10, 10 being the most important and 1 being the least. Total up the numbers from all the developers. Look at the item with the most points first, followed by the next. Schedule additional meetings if a deeper dialog is needed beyond the available time. If you run out of time in the meeting, save the remaining items for the next meeting.

Create action items from your conversations. During the planning phase, use this list to create tasks and influence your decision-making.

We've reached the end of our development cycle. From here, we just repeat the process, making improvements each pass. You won't have to think too much about the details as the team gets more comfortable. Everything operates on autopilot.

Now, let's talk about a typical day for a developer.

A Day in the Life

All our preparation and planning paid off with a productive and uninhibited workday for our team. We've built a process where the developer is free to concentrate on their work without having to think about the development flow. This is important because interruptions break concentration, causing both frustration and exhaustion. Sometimes, these interruptions can ruin productivity for an entire day.

We aren't saying developers are coding machines, working tirelessly for eight full hours. They need occasional breaks and time away from their screens to let their subconscious work. That downtime is often when their brains do the most work, connecting dots and formulating solutions.

The key for us as managers is removing all barriers when developers are coding. That way, downtime can be beneficial rather than an escape from constant interruption. By providing a daily process for each developer, we hope to provide even more structure to their day. This section discusses that process.

Starting Work

When the workday begins, each developer should take a moment before they start coding to review all messages and notifications. Since our team is remote and works synchronously, development likely continues even after a developer signs off for the day. Looking at all forms of communication can help others and get a developer up to date with anything that came up while they were away.

The following is a checklist you can provide your team to help them cover all places they receive communication.

- Read all unread emails.

- Review all real-time chat messages and notifications.

- Read missed conversations in shared real-time chat channels.

- Review GitHub notifications in either email, real-time chat, or the GitHub web UI.

- Review project management tool updates and comments.

- Review the current task or get a new task.

- Post and review standup messages or attend a standup meeting.

If the team finds there are too many notifications or messages to review, have them configure each service to filter out messages that don't concern them. Creating new channels in your real-time chat or email aliases is another way to gain finer-grained control over who receives certain notifications.

Ideally, we want all notifications and messages a developer receives to be relevant to them. One hundred percent relevancy isn't possible; some noise makes it through the filters. We don't want the team to receive so many messages that they ignore most of them. If this happens, they inevitably miss the important updates. Let's look at each type of communication a developer may receive and how it affects the team.

Updates on pull requests should be looked at as soon as possible to prevent the conversations from going stale. When a conversation stagnates, it prevents other developers from finishing their work. If a developer is too busy to provide feedback, have them reassign it to a new reviewer.

Our project management tool is another important place where conversations happen. Often, tasks need further clarifications or changes before they can be completed. Review ongoing conversations like comments, updates, and task assignments to keep work and planning moving forward.

Email and real-time chat are where longer conversations occur. Taking the time to review these messages can provide important context for the workday.

Reviewing these services before starting gives the developer time to think about their upcoming day. It's a refresher for what they worked on and helps them plan what they will be working on. It also brings any issues to the forefront so they can be shared during standup before everyone else is deep into their work.

Feel free to add or change our suggested list. Some real-time chat tools like Slack have plugins that allow a custom daily message to be sent. It is an easy way to automate the process and improve team adoption.

We are ready to work; let's move on to the developer workday.

Workday

We need each developer to do their part to keep the team moving forward and connected. Software development can be a messy process, filled with conflicts and problems. One of the more common conflicts is the code conflict. This happens when two people attempt to change the same line of code at the same time.

Git does a really good job at handling most conflicts and attempting to merge changes automatically. When conflicts can't be resolved, manual intervention is required. A capable diff tool makes resolving code conflicts possible but tedious.

Ideally, we want to avoid these conflicts when possible. We can do this using two different techniques. The first technique uses a branching strategy to promote a workflow that keeps production running smoothly while not blocking development. The other is a process that keeps our feature branches up to date with the latest changes from development. Let's look at the Git branching strategy first.

A Git branching strategy is a defined process for creating and merging branches. Without a strategy, knowing which branch is the "main" branch will be impossible. Figure 6-1 is a visual representation of a Git branching strategy using two stable branches and feature and release branches.

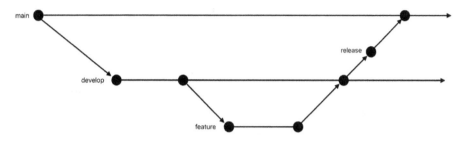

***Figure 6-1.** Git branching strategy*

We started our branching strategy by creating a "develop" branch from the "main" branch. The "develop" branch is where bleeding-edge development is committed, and the "main" branch reflects our stable production environment. When developers work on a task, they create a branch of the "develop" branch called a feature branch. Changes are made to this branch instead of directly to the "develop" branch.

When work is complete, create a pull request in GitHub to merge the changes into the "develop" branch. Other developers review and approve the changes, and only after a review can they be merged. This helps prevent bugs from slipping into the application.

Since our development environment is configured to deploy automatically upon merge to the "develop" branch, the changes are available for review by the original request on the development environment. You can use squash merging to condense commits into a single commit, but avoid rebase merging pull requests. Rebase merges are risky and can rewrite history when misused. In the worst case, a developer rebase merges and erases commits made by other developers, losing work. Also, don't squash merge release branches into the main since it messes with the history, making hotfix branches impossible.

Release branches and hotfixes are covered in an upcoming section, but these are the basics of our branch strategy. Come up with a naming schema for your feature branches. The "initials/description" or "cd/add_new_ui" pattern can inform the team who authored the branch and a provide a summary of the changes. It is also helpful when cleaning up old branches.

Another way to avoid conflicts is to keep feature branches updated with the latest changes on the "develop" branch, which receives updates from the entire team. Updating a feature branch often can catch or avoid conflicts, especially when performed at the beginning of the workday.

These are the Git commands to update a feature branch with the current "develop" branch changes. Make sure all local changes on the feature branch are committed and pushed to GitHub before running these commands in case problems occur when merging.

```
git checkout develop
git pull origin develop
git checkout feature_branch
git merge develop
```

If there are conflicts, use a differencing and merging tool like Meld or WinMerge to fix them, and then run the following commands.

```
git add conflicted_file.ext
git commit
```

If the developer is continuing work from a previous workday, perform these actions on the feature branch before making changes. That way, they are working with the latest and greatest code and aren't surprised by changes made while they are away. If possible, update feature branches throughout the day.

Now that your feature branch is ready, the developer can start their day. There are some additional tasks a developer needs to complete throughout the day. You can give your team the following list to help them remember those tasks.

- Monitor Slack for conversations and notifications.

- Respond to feedback on GitHub.

- Respond to feedback and updates on your project management tool.

- Periodically check email.

These tasks can be done during downtime. Developers aren't expected to respond to every notification immediately. They should use judgment to decide which items require prompt action and which do not. Unblocking other developers and fixing production problems should be a higher priority. A review request on a pull request is important but not as high.

How your team handles production support depends on the size. For small teams, monitoring and responding to production issues are most likely shared by everyone. Larger teams either have a support rotation or hire additional people to provide the level of support required for the application. Make a choice based on your current needs, but at some point, you should consider having a team other than your development team support day-to-day system operations.

Now, the developer is free to work however they see fit. When a task is complete, create a pull request on GitHub. A pull request signals the team's intent to merge changes into the development branch and eventually release them to production.

Once a pull request is created, the developer should perform the following actions.

1. Make sure all required status checks pass.

2. Assign one or more team members as reviewers.

3. Add appropriate labels.

4. Send a link to the pull request to reviewers.

Reviewers look at the pull request and provide feedback. The requester needs to address the feedback and possibly make changes to their branch. Once the pull request is approved, the developer should take the following actions.

1. Merge pull requests into the "develop" branch.

2. Wait for deployment to the development environment.

3. Review changes in the development environment.

4. Do the following if the development environment is broken.

    a. Create a new branch of the "develop" branch.

    b. Fix the issue.

    c. Create a new pull request in the "develop" branch.

    d. Go through the pull request review process.

    e. Merge the pull request.

    f. Check the development environment to confirm the fix.

5. Depending on the production deployment process, the developer may deploy to production.

The developer marks the task complete in the project management tool and takes the next task on the backlog. Since the tasks are prioritized during planning, they'll take the one on the top of the stack. If the developer cannot perform the work for that task, continue down the backlog until they find an appropriate task.

Eventually, the workday will end. Before signing off, a developer needs to do a few things to tie up their work. The next section discusses how to wrap up the day in a way that prepares for tomorrow.

The End of the Workday

The workday is over, and it's time to bring our work to a close. A developer may be tempted to code up to the eighth hour and then shut their laptops, signaling the end of work. Stopping abruptly often leads to a slow start the next day as we try to remember what we did the previous day. Add more time, like a weekend, and a developer will likely spend a significant amount of time Monday morning trying to remember what they did on Friday.

Instead, the team should spend time wrapping up the day as neatly as possible. It doesn't take a lot of effort. The result is a virtual desk that is ready to go when they sign back on. We also prevent blocking other team members on shared tasks.

To help your team remember to start this wind-down process, configure your real-time chat to notify them before they finish working. Like the morning to-do, this notification provides the end-of-day checklist, making it harder to forget.

Here is a list of items that need to be completed at the end of the workday.

- Get code to committable state and commit it.

- Merge the "develop" branch into the "feature" branch.

- Push feature branch changes to GitHub.

- Check email and respond to important emails.

- Check real-time chat and respond to import messages.

- Check the project management tool, update task progress, and respond to feedback.

- Make sure there aren't any production problems.

If the developer is unable to get their code into a committable state, they can leave their branch as is for the next day. This is not ideal and can be mitigated by making smaller commits throughout the day. Another option is to make a work-in-progress commit, even if the code is unfinished. GitHub allows pull requests to be merged using a squash merge to clean up Git history and hide work-in-progress commits. When the developer performs a squash merge, Git history shows a single commit for the entire pull request.

Now, the developer is ready to finish their work. All communications have been answered, and their environment is set up for tomorrow. A lot of work has gone into creating new features. Let's examine how to get this work to production to benefit our users.

Deploying to Production

It takes a lot of work to prepare our code for release to production. Planning, writing tests, paired programming, peer review, and automated checks are important for vetting new code and preventing bugs. When the code is finally ready, we want the deployment process to be as easy as possible.

Complicated, manual deployments are stressful and error-prone. Chapter 4 touched on using a platform as a service (Paas) to make deploying easy to set up and even easier to use. If you decide to use Paas, most of this section has already been handled.

If your deployment becomes complicated in the future, take the time to automate the manual steps. If that isn't possible, do your best to document the deployment process thoroughly.

When and how often you deploy is up to you and your company's needs. No matter your choice, status checks, a robust test suite, and an automated deployment process give you the confidence to deploy as many times as needed throughout the day. There is no right time to deploy. Some teams only need to deploy once per week or at the end of a sprint, while others need to deploy after each pull request merge.

We only have one rule we recommend you follow. Refrain from deploying on Friday or whatever day is the last workday before the weekend. Deploying on Fridays opens the team up to overtime and burnout when something goes wrong. If you've worked in software long enough, you've experienced the pain of deploying on Friday and having your weekend plans ruined. Instead of risking disaster, wait for Monday to deploy. Your team will appreciate it.

Once you decide on a release schedule, there are a few other items we need to have in place before releasing.

- A process to migrate your database and roll back changes

- If required, a process to place your application in maintenance mode during deployment

- Database backup when major database changes are being made (Your team may choose to perform a backup on every deployment if it is fast enough. Incremental and differential backups can also speed up backup times by only backing up what's changed since the last full backup.)

- Deploy notifications on real-time chat

- Scripts or tools to invalidate caches or restart services after deploying

If a deployment is a one-way, non-reversible operation, take extra care to prepare and backup data. All other deployments should be reversible with the click of a button or a single command.

Setting this up takes work, but the effort is worth it. When a developer isn't scared to deploy, it removes pressure from the team. The team won't be afraid to move fast, and the company will benefit from this.

Let's move on to the actual deployment process.

Deploy Process

Deploying should be a repeatable process that doesn't change. The same steps are performed in a defined order until the deployment is complete. This section lays out the steps. If you are using Paas, deployment automation is handled. You must roll your own if you use a cloud service provider.

Palumi and Terraform provide a way to represent your cloud infrastructure as code. You can use commands to create, update, and destroy assets. You can often re-create your systems in minutes using a database backup and a few commands. If you deployed your application to a virtualized server like AWS EC2, you would need a tool to handle configuration. As of the writing of this book, Ansible is a popular tool for handling this. You can use it to configure your servers and automate deployment.

Let's step through what a production deployment should look like.

- Before we start, you must be able to answer "yes" to the following questions.

  - Is the development environment working without issue?

  - Do all tests pass on the "develop" branch (this can be tested when creating a release branch and pull request)?

  - Are no deploys happening currently?

- Call out intent to release to production on real-time chat.

- Create a release branch. Use the recommended release_YYYYMMDD format. Append a-z to the end for multiple release branches per day.

- Create a pull request for the release branch to be added to the main.

  - Provide release notes of what changed.

  - Have another developer review the pull request.

  - Make sure status checks pass.

- Merge pull requests into the "main" branch. Do not squash merge because this causes problems with history, making it difficult to merge hotfix branches.

- Monitor automatic deployment or manual trigger deployment using commands.

- Confirm that the deployment was successful. You can manually check the site, monitor the observability platform, or listen for alarms.

That's it. Most of the work done to automate deploying should make your deployment straightforward. If your deployment becomes complicated at any point, fix it as soon as possible. When the fear of deploying creeps into your team, it's hard to undo it.

A hotfix can be deployed in response if a deployment causes a problem that needs an immediate fix. Hotfixes are helpful when the "develop" branch is not ready for deployment, but a bug fix can't wait. Creating a hotfix is like creating a release. The difference is we branch off "main" instead of "develop". The steps to do this are as follows.

1. Create a hotfix branch off "main". Use the recommended hotfix_YYYYMMDD format. Append a-z to the end for multiple hotfix branches per day.

2. Make the changes to fix the problem.

3. Commit changes.

4. Push changes to GitHub.

5. Create a pull request to merge the branch into both "main" and "develop."

6. Make sure all status checks pass.

7. Request a review and get approved.

8. Merge into main to deploy to production and then merge into the "develop" branch to make sure changes don't get removed on the next deploy.

We've completed our full development cycle, which started with planning and ended with a release to production. But what happens when something goes wrong long after a deployment? Let's look at that now.

Putting out Fires

Even with our planning and due diligence, unexpected failures may happen. It might not even be anything the team did. AWS is a very reliable service, but it still fails from time to time. It might not be a system-wide failure. At times, individual services experience downgraded availability and function in unexpected ways. When AWS experiences problems, our application and our users are affected.

A procedure is needed to handle problems with our production environment. Handling issues in an unstructured way means that a select few—the team's most senior developers—are accountable for the entire system.

Leaving system reliability to our senior developers can lead to burnout. It also means less time for them to perform important tasks like building frameworks, leading projects, mentoring junior developers, and focusing on challenging assignments.

Since the team knows the ins and outs of the application, they often are responsible for ensuring it runs smoothly. As the company grows and uptime becomes key, this approach doesn't scale. Hiring people to provide infrastructure and support is key to avoiding overburdening your team with too many responsibilities. Some services can provide after-hours support if hiring a dedicated support team isn't financially viable.

The development team can troubleshoot and fix issues as they arise. You and high-level management determine how the team responds to issues. Create a severity scale to assess problems and determine how the team should react.

The following is an example of issue levels.

- **Critical**: The entire application has crashed.

- **Major**: A serious bug in software is affecting most users.

- **Minor**: A bug causes minor inconvenience to users.

From here, you should decide on a reasonable resolution time for each level. This can be determined by the company's financial impact for each level. For example, the team might be required to respond within 15 minutes of a critical issue occurring because a critical issue may cause serious financial setbacks for the company. Minor problems like bugs that are slight annoyances for users can be handled when there is time in the schedule.

Everyone at the company must respect the scale and avoid labeling every issue as a critical, show-stopping problem. If all bugs are labeled critical, even if they aren't, the scale loses all meaning.

Some problems are apparent, like an HTTP 500 response from the web server, while others are not. Bugs encountered by users are less noticeable. Without the proper reporting, the team may never know whether users are experiencing issues with the application.

In the previous chapter, we set up monitoring and alarms. Your alarms should be configured to email or message the team on real-time chat whenever a system anomaly is detected or the site crashes. If you've signed up for an observability platform like Airbrake, the system can notify you of production errors. If your users can report bugs, configure the bug reporting system to notify the team via email.

We want the flow of information to be delivered in a way that is not too noisy but still visible. Since our real-time chat is the tool our developers look at the most throughout the workday, having a notifications channel is a good way for them to keep an eye on production.

When a problem occurs, whoever sees it first should report it to the team so whoever is responsible can investigate it. Otherwise, the problem could go unnoticed, which could happen very easily with a remote team.

Now that the problem has been identified, someone needs to take point. This can be done by whoever is best equipped or available to handle it. Or it can be assigned by you. If you have a person assigned to support rotation, as explained in the next section, they would be the one. Make sure you don't put the same person on every problem. It is a quick way to burn a developer out.

Starting an incident room on a video conference and posting the link in the engineering chat is an easy way to get others involved. Not everyone in the incident room needs to be actively fixing the problem, but having more people involved can spark a conversation that leads to a fix. It's also good exposure for junior developers to understand how problems get solved. The person on point can even assign tasks to people in the incident room to investigate.

Once the problem is fixed and the solution deployed, document any important information about the fix. Having an incident report and performing a root cause analysis can help formalize the process around incidents. You can then use the report to help document common problems and fixes on your wiki, which can help other developers experiencing similar issues.

Support Rotation

Applications need constant maintenance to run smoothly. Refactoring, software updates, building tools, and fixing non-priority bugs are easy to ignore until they become a problem. Having a developer assigned to a support rotation can allow them to work on these tasks while handling production issues. The team can take turns being in this role. If the team stays on top of the maintenance, they won't fall behind.

Support rotation differs from on-call support, where a developer is available after hours to handle issues. We define support as a period of a week or two where a developer prioritizes maintenance tasks and fixing problems. It doesn't mean the developer has to be available 24/7 for support. If you need 24/7 support, we suggest staffing accordingly or hiring a third-party service. Placing support duty on developers can easily burn your team out and lower velocity. Some developers won't even consider your company if you have an on-call rotation. Plan accordingly for your business needs.

Looking Ahead

Crossing your fingers and hoping problems don't happen is not an effective approach to software development. Getting ahead of technical debt and preventing bugs requires effort. No matter where we are in the development lifecycle, we need to think about the future.

Having a proactive mindset means considering other developers and how the choices we make today may affect them in the future. If we only write code for today, future projects can pay the price—including missed deadlines, buggier code, and frustrated developers.

Every task and every pull request are opportunities to consider how we can improve what's already there. Deciding to do a little more instead of making a quick change can go a long way toward improving the quality of the code.

You should write code like you are building a library for external developers. This means we need the following to be effective.

- Detailed documentation with examples

- Ability to change functionality through configuration

- Code designed to be used like building blocks, giving the developer the power to assemble custom solutions

- Easy-to-understand interface

If you've made your code public, you wouldn't require the developer to read every line of code to use it. You would expect them to be able to drop the library into their application and start using it. If that is true, then we shouldn't ask that of our internal team.

What are some of the ways we can look ahead? Here are some ideas.

- Add time for refactoring. This can include refactoring legacy or new code as it's being written.

- Always write tests, especially for bugs. In the future, you can expand testing to security and integration tests.

- Build frameworks, not one-off fixes for tasks.

- As your application gets bigger, move functionality to separate libraries.

- Documentation for everything: you can always delete what you don't use, but it's difficult to remember what you've forgotten.

- Make time to automate manual processes.

  - Write scripts for common tasks.

  - Build web tools to handle jobs usually done by developers.

- Slow down the review process. Consider code changes and how they will affect the system. Break up bigger pull requests into smaller ones for more effective reviews.

Plenty of books can teach you good programming practices that avoid code rot. The focus of this book isn't to teach you how to write better code. We want you and your team to always understand how the decisions they make today affect future development. There won't always be the luxury of time to do things the best way. Corners will be cut to meet deadlines. Those cut corners won't be felt immediately. Instead, they may appear when you least expect them. A task takes longer than expected, and a project runs over a deadline. Parts of the application become fragile and error-prone.

When we include improvement as part of our regular schedule, we chip away at these problems little by little. We restructured the inefficient code to make it easier to work with. Finally, we create robust systems that expect errors and handle them predictably.

Roles and Responsibilities

Software development is a broad field. Even within web development, developers can have specialized skills and varied experience. Front-end engineers, for example, build single-page applications that run in the browser, while a site reliability engineer builds tools to manage infrastructure. Both are very different roles and are very important to the team's function. Generalists know a little about everything. Treating every developer as interchangeable parts of the software development machine won't always work.

There is a lot to consider when building and operating a team. Experience and personalities play a big part in what tasks a developer can perform. Senior developers can build frameworks and solve complex problems, while junior developers can focus on smaller tasks, working within a defined structure. Some will lead, while others will follow. Not everyone is able to perform every function on a team. What's important is that each person knows their role and what's expected from them.

If the team can support it, roles can change from sprint to sprint. If you plan to do this, call out what part of the system or type of work a developer handles for the sprint. If your team is all generalists, this step is probably not needed.

Roles aren't fixed. As developers grow, they gain the experience and knowledge to fulfill different roles. During one-on-ones, review how a developer is fulfilling their current roles. Discuss what they can do to improve. Work with them to help them grow into other roles they are interested in. Pair them with other developers who already have the desired skills. For example, a junior developer can work with a senior developer, building new frameworks for the team. A back-end developer can pair with a front-end developer to learn about JavaScript.

Create a plan and follow up. If we don't put in the effort to grow our team, people will stagnate and get bored. Encourage growth and make a part of the process.

Summary

This chapter examined a typical developer workweek. The Agile methodology was used to handle change by grouping work into sprints. This process allows our team to iterate on ideas quickly and provides the flexibility needed to build web applications.

Before a sprint begins, we plan. During the planning phase, we conceptualize new projects, fill in existing project details, and finalize tasks for the coming sprints. After the sprint, we reviewed how we did as a team. Dialogs about successes and failures during a sprint allow our team to fine-tune their productivity.

Looking ahead can set the team up for long-term success. By building extendable systems, we provide building blocks that slowly grow over time.

Properly defining our teams' roles and responsibilities can avoid confusion. The next chapter delves into how to structure our teams into small, efficient teams.

CHAPTER 7

The Strike Team

Our ecosystem is set up and ready to go. We have a development process in place to burn through all those tasks in our backlog. All we need is a team of talented people ready to design and build our application. But before we start the hiring process by posting job listings and performing interviews, we must consider how we plan to structure our team.

Why do we need a team structure? Can't we create a massive backlog of tasks, hire as many developers as possible, and let them have at it? This approach can work for a small team consisting of a few developers. Since the team is small, keeping everyone in sync doesn't require much effort. Problems happen once you grow beyond a small team and need to manage multiple projects.

Imagine a team consisting of two people. For this team, communication is limited to a single line, from person A to person B. Hire another person, and you now have three people. That means there are three distinct lines of communication—still very manageable.

As we add more people, the number of lines of communication grows quickly.

- 4 developers = 6 lines of communication

- 6 developers = 15 lines of communication

- 12 developers = 66 lines of communication

- 24 developers = 276 lines of communication

© Carleton DiLeo, Jennifer Reyes 2025
C. DiLeo and J. Reyes, *Effective Remote Teams*,
https://doi.org/10.1007/979-8-8688-1303-0_7

By the time there is a team of two dozen people, which is not uncommon for a modern software company, the lines of communication balloon to 276. Without any resemblance of organization, keeping communication from breaking down is futile. There are just too many people with too many possible interactions.

As our team grows, the communication vectors between people begin to resemble a complex mesh network (Figure 7-1). Each new person increases the effort needed to manage the team. There comes a point where further growth becomes unsustainable. Communication deteriorates, and getting anything done becomes an agonizingly slow affair.

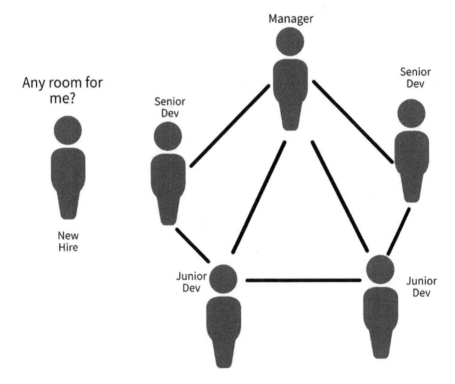

Figure 7-1. *Communication complexity*

You'll need a solution to avoid burnout and limit confusion. One solution is limiting our team size to a finite number, which only works for so long. The company's needs will eventually grow beyond what the team can handle. We need a way to structure our engineering department to allow growth.

This chapter discusses organizing our developers into strike teams that operate independently with minimal oversight from managers. Much like the mesh network, a single developer is in charge of a group of other developers. This person acts like a router, managing communication internally and collecting, filtering, and forwarding only relevant messages from their team to other teams who may find them appropriate. The strike team is a simple but effective concept. It can scale to large teams and is easy to set up.

Strike teams can work independently on projects without overwhelming you with details. This frees up your time to think about the future and be available for your employees. Let's start forming our team by establishing the key resource that keeps it all together: the leader.

Follow the Leader

No team is fully operational from inception. It takes time for everyone to get their footing, understand the technology stack, and feel comfortable working within a process. Like starting a new job, everything is new all at once.

When starting development on a new application, there are so many unknowns. The founders have ideas of what they want to build, but until we start coding, the final product is just a vague concept living in our heads. As time passes and we push out new features, we begin to form a picture of what the application will become. Sometimes, what we ship to users is very different from the initial paper napkin design created in the beginning.

Many ideas we thought were correct back turned out to be wrong or not like we imagined. Since we are using the Agile methodology, these missteps are acceptable. We can always change our minds and pivot after a sprint. Mistakes only set us back a little bit.

Unfortunately, the first lines of code we write are a different story. Early design decisions affect development well into the future. If our initial system is brittle and inflexible to change, every additional line of code we write compounds the problem. There will be a point when the simplest changes take a disproportionate amount of time.

When we decide to refactor, we are met with resistance because our code does not support the ability to make incremental changes. Making improvements means a full-blown rewrite is required. Application rewrites are a hard sell for a new company trying to build steady revenue. Stopping development for months for no gain other than to fix past mistakes isn't financially viable. We are forced to keep the code as is and factor in additional time and frustration as just a part of everyday life for the team.

Making thoughtful decisions with our code, especially in the beginning, pays dividends in the future. Every corner cut in the name of "just getting it done" adds to our technical debt. Sometimes, these choices are unavoidable. Hacking together a solution to acquire a new customer that keeps the lights on is worth the debt it incurs. After all, if the company folds, no amount of technical debt will matter. It gets dangerous when this type of development becomes the norm. We must balance the good and the bad to move the company forward without jeopardizing future development. We should make calculated decisions vs. pretending our actions don't have consequences. There comes a day when we must pay off our technical debt; it may not be a time when we are willing to do it.

Imagine a developer tasked with developing a feature that could make or break a massive business opportunity. The project is estimated to take one month, but after deeper investigation, several problems may cause it to take much longer. An underlying system that was hastily put together last year must be completely rewritten to make the new feature work. No hack or workaround will solve the problem. What should be a straightforward change has turned into a larger undertaking—from a choice made a year ago.

It is important to start building frameworks and designing code that is extendible rather than complete tasks as one-off quick fixes. That initial effort helps us get faster rather than slowing down as the code grows.

This development approach can be read about in books, but only through trial and error does a developer learn what techniques work and what don't. Applying theory to real-world solutions allows developers to shape their thinking over time. Our first hires should be experienced developers. They are the ones to lay the groundwork that determines future development. Pulling from their experience to build a stable platform gives our team a better chance for success.

Hire senior-level or higher developers with experience building complex applications. They should know how to develop frameworks and libraries. These first hires should have a strong sense of direction and only require a little oversight on projects. Giving vague concepts and weak task definitions shouldn't stop them from completing work. Instead, they can make decisions and move on with a plan to refactor and improve these shortcomings later.

We recommend focusing on open-ended questions for the interview that foster deeper discussions about code practices. Being able to recite memorized facts about a specific language or framework won't allow us to understand how a developer solves problems. We want to know their opinions and understand if they align with ours. Knowing how a developer responds to a situation where they have little help or direction is vital for the early days of the application when it's a struggle to get to a stable MVP.

Here are some examples of topics you can discuss during an interview.

- Opinions on coding best practices

- Experience developing new systems

- Initial design process

- Implementation process

- Knowing when to make cuts

- Refactoring

- Managing business needs vs. engineering needs

- Handling the disconnected aspect of remote development

- Providing product definition feedback

These are some examples to get a conversation going. Once it starts, avoid steering it too much. Let the interviewee guide the discussion and have them share rather than you asking. This approach provides a deeper insight into their thoughts and helps you understand if they will be a good fit. These developers pave the way for the application and become the team's foundation. Knowing how they will handle that is essential.

With the hiring process underway, we need to think about how to set up the team once we've started making offers and bringing people on board.

The Setup

Let's start with a small group of knowledgeable developers who will build the application's roots. During this time, your team meets often to discuss designs and vet ideas, attempting to understand how they will affect the team now and in the future.

Our team will build wide, not deep. Initially, our application will resemble the wooden framework of a house. The frame is constructed first. You can tell it's a house, but the details haven't been finalized. It's empty—the electrical and plumbing need to be installed after the insulation, the walls, and the flooring. Layer by layer, everything is placed until the house is finished.

Building an application follows a similar approach. We start with a framework and slowly fill in all the empty parts. We defer decisions on the most minor details until the last possible moment. Modifications can be made to the framework, but it largely resembles the structure we first built.

Our senior developers, chosen for their expertise, are the architects of our application. Once they've established the foundation, we hire less experienced developers to assist. With their extensive knowledge, the senior developer acts as the strike team leader. A strike team (Figure 7-2) is a small team of roughly three to five people that operates independently from the rest of engineering. The strike team leader bridges the team, management, and the other strike teams. A strike team consists of junior to mid-level developers. They are an independent unit that works on their own projects. When you have multiple teams, the strike team leader can host the sprint planning meeting and the weekly sync for their team.

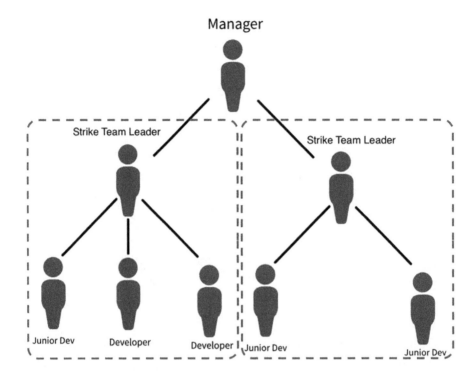

Figure 7-2. *Strike team organization chart*

All the developers on the strike team still report to the hiring manager. The manager is responsible for their career growth, HR issues, and one-on-one meetings. The strike team leader handles the day-to-day communication related to a project.

Instead of the manager fielding every question and having the final say on all decisions, the strike team leader is responsible. They handle most things before involving the manager, reducing the manager's involvement and allowing them to focus on other big-picture work.

The strike team leader is responsible for the following.

- Setting technical direction

- Designing the initial frameworks

- Overseeing documentation

- Overseeing code created for a project

- Assigning tasks to their team

The manager provides high-level project direction, meeting with the senior developer to answer questions and discuss technical viability. As the manager, you must listen and determine how all the projects fit into the bigger vision. You don't need to know how exactly each part works; you only need to understand how the final product operates from the user's perspective. Coupling that with your understanding of the business, you make decisions beyond what the strike team leader does, allowing them to focus on their projects.

For example, you might not understand user authentication's technical details, but you know a username and password are required to gain access. You know that all passwords are encrypted using industry standards, and compliance is maintained for the user's data.

The other details aren't crucial for your job. On the other hand, the strike team leader understands precisely how the systems they build work. They are the ones giving the final call on technical details. Their team looks to them to answer complex technical questions. The strike team leader looks to the manager to make a hard call on which features can be cut when a project is running behind.

The freedom and trust between you and your strike team leaders is a pillar that allows both of you to focus on your job. They have the time and focus to solve hard problems while you have the time to plan for the future. This trust empowers them to handle the day-to-day decision-making, giving you back valuable time to think long-term and handle unexpected problems.

If you want a formal process for receiving updates from your teams, set up monthly meetings with strike team leaders to review proposed designs and answer questions. Make sure to stay within the bounds. If you are technical, it's easy to slip into old habits and find yourself deep in the nitty-gritty technical design talk. Trust in your team leaders and let them handle the day-to-day. It provides you more time to be an effective manager.

With your strike team leader hired, let's move on with filling out the team with the developers who handle the bulk of the work.

The Workers

You can hire less experienced developers once a senior developer has been hired and has had time to understand the application and build some of the foundational code. Even with only a single developer, you can start building a team using the structure provided in the past section. Getting used to the structure now makes it easier to build upon it when things get busy.

The junior and mid-level developers are the team's heavy lifters. They often write the most lines of code and complete more tasks than a senior developer. They're less experienced, a mix of mid-level and junior developers, but they have a solid understanding of software development foundations. They work within established frameworks and processes, focusing on the code needed to complete a task. They are still responsible for delivering high-quality, tested code, but their focus is at a function and class level rather than system-wide.

For example, if a senior developer built a framework for importing data into the database, the workers would be the ones to implement many of the classes performing the data loading. The senior developer would create a list of all the different types of data to be loaded. Then, workers would implement each step using the documentation produced by the senior developer. The classes they build handle the details for loading files, parsing data, and formatting it to the required format, all within the established guidelines. The junior developer doesn't need to know best practices for ETLs (extract, transform, load), only how to follow instructions and write clear, tested code.

The junior developers can hone their skills through their own focused work. They can experiment with different class structures, variable naming, design patterns, etc. As long as the implementation fits within the strike team leader plan, it's okay.

There is also room for mentorship for junior and mid-level developers. A strike team is small, so the senior developer can make time to pair programs and lead design discussions. Paired with a defined career path and one-on-one meetings, developers can grow into different roles, maybe even becoming strike team leaders one day.

Next, we'll talk about how to handle decision-making.

Making Decisions

Decisions are made at every level of the company. Everyone, from the CEO to the junior developer, has a role and specific responsibilities. Each person's decisions affect the company in some way. What differs is the impact. CEOs make a few far-reaching decisions that take time to decide. Choices at this level can have profound financial implications for years to come. Junior developers make many quick, smaller decisions that are felt immediately. Their choices are the difference between a new feature working or not.

All these decisions matter to the company's success, but they are devoid of each person's intimate knowledge of the situation. The CEO doesn't require approval from every employee to set a new company direction, and in turn, the employees don't need the CEO's sign-off on every task. It's not a feasible approach to running a company. There wouldn't be enough time in the day. Companies in other industries don't handle decision-making this way, nor should we. This goes double for your team.

It's not that your team's input isn't valuable. Even the most inexperienced developers can provide important insight into problems outside their skill level. The problem is that, for the occasional nugget of wisdom, we put undue stress on them. We are asking them to share the responsibility of more skilled and experienced team members who have had years to build their skills.

Imagine being a junior developer who just got hired. They struggle to understand the code and process and put all the theories they've learned into practice. You've asked the whole team to brainstorm possible project ideas for the team to fill out the end-of-year roadmap. Nowhere in their job description does it list project planning and roadmap, but they are being asked to take on that role.

Expectations need to be set so everyone knows what their job entails. Going beyond that description is fine when focused on career growth. Pushing outside our comfort level is how we improve and learn new skills.

At some point, we must draw a line and remember everyone has a job to fulfill. Everyone needs the time and freedom to explore that job to be successful. Constant interruptions eat into that time.

Decision-making happens at different levels. Depending on your team, these levels may differ from what we've provided.

The following is an example of a three-level structure.

- **High level**: This level involves project planning and prioritization. Decide what team works on which project. Determine project priority. Make changes to processes.

- **System level**: Decide and design framework infrastructure and provide technical vision. Determine which libraries to adopt. Set coding standards.

- **Task level**: Decide what code is needed to complete a task.

At the high level, you, the manager, decide what projects will be worked on. You create a roadmap with the product team. You make the final call on features for a project. You develop new processes to fix what's not working and change existing ones to fit your team dynamic. You may also meet regularly with your strike team leaders to hash out project details and get feedback.

The senior developers or strike team leaders handle the system level. It's their job to translate the company's needs into a fully functioning system. They decide what frameworks to build, which libraries to adopt, and what the application code should look like. They guide projects to completion. They field questions and mentor the developers on their team.

The product team works at the system level, fleshing out each project with tasks and features and working iteratively. Their job is to design the application's look and feel and determine how it functions, considering user feedback. They iterate week after week, making decisions without developer involvement unless needed. Once task definitions are complete, developer feedback is considered and factored into the final task.

The junior to mid-level developers, or the worker developers, work at the task level. They work on the tasks in the backlog, writing the code that makes the application function. As long as the code is well-tested and functions correctly, the naming, algorithms, and patterns are up to them to decide.

Working with Time Zones

Building a remote team offers a significant benefit to in-person. When hiring, you aren't restricted to people in your geographical region. You can hire from a wide range of locations. The available talent pool is much broader. The only requirement outside a matching skillset is access to a fast, reliable internet connection. This is an excellent opportunity to bring in diverse talent and fresh perspectives.

The biggest hurdle when working with people worldwide is dealing with time zones. When the time difference between team members becomes too large, the strain on the team may become significant. Most of the issue comes from coordinating tasks. In extreme situations, one team member will be going to sleep as another starts their day. Getting answers to questions and scheduling meetings becomes almost impossible unless one of the team members is willing to shift their schedule. People have lives outside of work, so this can be a hard ask. Many teams need at least a few hours of overlap between team members to work effectively.

While asynchronous communication can mitigate the problems caused by significant time-zone gaps, we will eventually want to meet over video. This is especially true for sprint planning meetings, which involve a lot of back-and-forth dialogs. Finding a time that works for everyone can mean some developers must attend the meeting at inconvenient times.

One solution to the time-zone problem is to limit hiring to a certain number of hours plus or minus from your time-zone. It solves the problem but limits who you can hire. If you want a wider talent pool selection, you can use the strike team structure to your advantage. Each team is a separate entity that operates mostly independently of you and the other teams. If the time zones for the developers and team leader are close enough, they can work without issue. As long as the strike team leaders live in a time zone within a reasonable offset from your own, meeting regularly for status updates won't be a problem.

Meetings involving the entire company happen infrequently, so asking employees to meet at awkward times is less of a problem. Waiting to have company meetings during the off-site can avoid this problem altogether if the company off-sites occur regularly.

Each strike team leader handles day-to-day communication and, in turn, provides updates to you. The strike team leaders are within a certain time zone within your reach, and their team is within a time zone within their scope. This approach extends the possible areas we can hire.

Most likely, you won't have to stretch this far to build your team, but it's an option that wouldn't otherwise be possible for an in-person team if needed. Find your tolerances when dealing with time zones. If the time difference becomes a strain, rethink your approach to managing your team. You don't need to be there for every meeting and each decision. Use your project management tool, email, and real-time chat to make communication more asynchronous.

Summary

This chapter explained how to structure a team. The strike team model provides a simple approach to building small, independent teams. It's easy to implement but provides a scalable way to grow. We can use this structure to delegate decisions and work around time-zone issues.

As we move forward, it's important to keep our eyes on the future. While completing all the planned work for a sprint is a team's top priority, we must also consider how what we do today affects the team in the future. Even with an effective team, the way we complete each task can ensure the speed and quality of our work doesn't degrade over time.

The next chapter focuses on how to handle change and growth.

PART IV

Keeping It Together

CHAPTER 8

Handling Change and Growth

Change is inevitable for any company. Building a successful product attracts more users, increasing demand for new features and bug fixes. It's a good problem to have. It's what co-founders dream about when their ideas are little more than drawings on a napkin.

While success is a good thing, there comes a point when there is too much work for a small team to handle. Project start dates get pushed further and further out as your team struggles to keep up. In the worst-case scenario, business opportunities fall through because vital features take too long to develop. If your team doesn't add more people, it may collapse under the strain.

Knowing when to grow isn't as simple as hiring as many developers as the company can afford. More people mean more complexity when planning and organizing projects. Hiring too quickly can result in a large team with insufficient work to keep them busy. As your team burns through money, workers become bored and disengaged. It's not an ideal scenario.

We want our team to always be engaged in work that delivers value to our customers and grows the business. This means a full roadmap with projects planned for six months to a year out.

© Carleton DiLeo, Jennifer Reyes 2025
C. DiLeo and J. Reyes, *Effective Remote Teams*,
https://doi.org/10.1007/979-8-8688-1303-0_8

This chapter helps you understand when to identify different signs that signal change is needed, what to look for, and how to respond to signs that something needs to change. We also discuss when to hire vs. when to upgrade your tool and process. Let's start with the signs of strain that tell us when it's time to look deeper.

Signs of Strain

No job is perfect. Pressures at work ebb and flow depending on potential opportunities and unforeseen problems. Working longer hours and pushing hard to get a project over the finish line happens from time to time in software development. For software developers, it's part of the job. Sometimes, there is downtime for research and exploration, while other times, we are laser-focused on a deadline.

Having these bursts of productivity is manageable when they are infrequent and short. Problems arise when there is little or no lull between these crunch periods. When a team experiences crunch period after crunch period, it won't take long before they burn out and people start leaving for more stable jobs.

We want to avoid burning out because losing team members is not ideal. When someone leaves, we lose institutional knowledge. We must also spend time and resources finding and training replacements.

Knowing the signs of strain early before they become big problems is important. If not, we will never be able to grow our team and tackle work that leads to company success.

Let's examine several pain points that can indicate a future problem. Use these as a warning sign. Like "code smells" in software development, they might not always lead to real problems but are important enough not to overlook.

Too Many Blockers

In Chapter 6, we set up a daily process where developers provide updates via daily scrum or standup meeting. This update required each person on the team to provide the following.

- What I did

- What I'm working on

- Blockers

The part of the update we are focusing on now is the blockers. Even a healthy team has a few blockers from time to time. No matter how much time you spend on it, planning will never be perfect. Oversights happen, and tasks overlap, but when developers are constantly waiting to move forward on tasks for one reason or another, this is a problem.

Pay close attention to the daily standups. If you notice the team reporting blockers almost daily, there might be a problem. Look into what is causing the blockers. Certain blockers are more problematic than others.

Here are some of the reasons a team might be blocked.

- Junior and mid-level developers waiting for direction from a senior developer

- Too many projects or tasks waiting on work from one developer

- Too many projects or tasks are waiting for definition from the Product team

- Projects or decisions waiting for approval

These blockers cause tasks to stall and take longer to complete. Developers start new tasks while they wait, increasing the number of in-progress tasks. Often, the sprint ends with a lot of incomplete work, and the incomplete tasks must be carried over to the next sprint. This ends up pushing out work planned for that sprint to the next. Projects get pushed out to later dates, and the problem continues.

There are a few reasons why these types of blockers happen. A single developer having too many responsibilities can cause a bottleneck. Problems with the product definition can be caused by insufficient processes or not having enough people on the product team. Finally, you could be a bottleneck if you are trying to fill too many roles.

In the early days of development, you'll often take on many roles instead of hiring a dedicated person to fill these roles. This works when your team is small. Once you grow and multiple projects are happening at once, you can find yourself not having enough time in the day to handle it all. As a result, your team ends up being blocked on tasks that need your input or approval.

Too Many High-Priority Projects

Your roadmap is a constant work in progress. Existing projects get reworked to improve clarity. New projects are conceptualized and added to a never-ending backlog. The lessons we learn after completing projects help shape the roadmap. The more we develop, the more we know and are better informed about making decisions.

While the roadmap is always a work in progress, ideally, we want to have about a year of work planned. The planned work on the roadmap should be able to be completed without significant overtime. If this is not the case, this is a sign that there is more work than the team can handle.

When there is too much work, projects that directly impact the company's financials start to pile up. Failing to complete priority projects on time can make or break business deals. If your company is venture capital-backed, the company's next round of funding could be jeopardized.

If these spikes in workload are infrequent, you might be able to ask your team to work more hours temporarily. Teams can usually handle a short-term work crunch of one to two weeks. When the workload decreases to normal levels, you can offer to compensate them with paid time off or a bonus if your company has the funds. If a short crunch isn't enough to bring the roadmap back to normal, you must hire more people.

Increased Workweek Hours

A *work crunch* is defined as a sustained workweek above the required 40 hours for a salaried employee. At its worst, a crunch can balloon to 80 hours for months at a time. These periods of long hours are very demanding and have long-term effects on a team if not remedied with appropriate time off.

At some point, the damage brought on by crunch can be irreversible. People will reach a breaking point and leave, further exacerbating the problem. It won't be long before the quality of the code is affected and bugs start popping up.

If you notice your team regularly working more than 40 hours per week, you have a problem. If working late nights to finalize tasks is the norm rather than the exception, that's a sign that there is too much work and insufficient people to complete it. You'll need to expand the team to lessen the burden.

Not everyone may be overworked. Sometimes, work is not spread evenly across the team, leaving some working more hours than others. Be mindful of developers who constantly put in overtime to unblock projects or get them across the finish line. This is a sign that an additional person who mirrors the work being done by that developer is needed. Sometimes, it may only take a single new hire to get the team back on track.

Too Many Bugs

An overworked team is more likely to make mistakes. Software development is mentally taxing. It requires deep focus and concentration to get right, and a tired mind can't keep everything needed in its head at once.

Fatigue is one reason why bug rates can increase. A team working in a fatigued state creates more bugs. Their tired brains might misinterpret tasks and mess up logic in the code, causing features not to function properly. The overall quality of the application slowly degrades, and users become frustrated, possibly moving to a more stable platform.

Another reason for increased bug rates is a lack of knowledge. A lack of knowledge can come from time constraints where developers aren't given enough time to properly explore a technology or new part of the code. They are then forced to make educated guesses based on a limited understanding of their tools. Often, these guesses are wrong, causing bugs.

Lack of knowledge also comes from inexperience from either limited years of professional programming experience or limited time working with a specific technology. For example, your team might be skilled back-end developers but only have limited experience working with front-end technology. If they are tasked with creating single-page apps using a framework like React, there is a steep learning curve. You will likely see more bugs coming from that front-end code during that time.

Here are some of the areas in which new teams often lack knowledge.

- Infrastructure

- Front end

- Design

- Database administration

- Customer support

- High-scale/high-availability design

This list depends on the type of application you are developing, but all new teams have blind spots that eventually need to be filled.

Velocity Slowdown

Depending on your project management tool, you may have access to team velocity reports. These reports show the amount of work a team completed in previous sprints. If so, you need to provide estimates for each task to take advantage of this feature. In the absence of automated reporting, manual reporting can be an alternative method to track velocity. You can use a spreadsheet to track the data.

Team velocity isn't constant. It fluctuates depending on many factors. You'll need to record the velocity for every sprint to determine trends and calculate averages. These data points are much more helpful than a single data point.

For example, let's suppose you tracked the number of story points completed for the last six sprints. You see that the number of points completed varies slightly from sprint to sprint, but overall, it stays within a range of 26 to 33 (Figure 8-1).

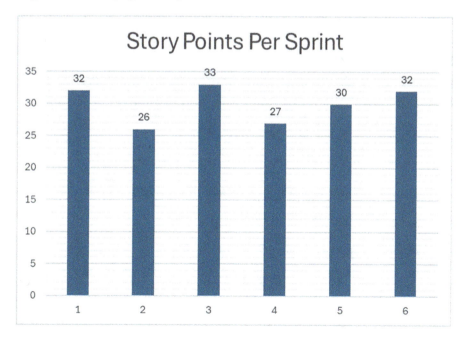

Figure 8-1. *Story points per sprint*

If we compute the average, we determine that the team completes about 30 story points per sprint. That means we can plan for about 30 points of work per sprint. If we also collect velocity at the developer level, we could even determine how much velocity will drop during a developer's time off.

Do not use these velocity totals to measure individual performance. Productivity is more than their total velocity. Developers perform many tasks, like code reviews, pair programming, and attending meetings, which are not tracked in the project management tool. Penalizing a developer for a velocity that doesn't meet a certain number may lead to them inflating their estimates to fix it. Ultimately, you lose a valuable tool for planning for little gain.

Collecting velocity data can be used to detect drops in team velocity. If we know the average velocity, we can spot significant and persistent dips in productivity. For example, let's use the average velocity displayed in Figure 8-1. You continued to collect velocity numbers and noticed velocity totals had dropped to 20 story points per sprint. That is a 33% drop in productivity. Since the drop has persisted for multiple sprints, there is likely a problem that must be fixed to return velocity to its previous state.

Once you've identified a problem, you must find the cause. Here are some possible situations that can cause drops in velocity.

- Developers taking paid time off or sick leave

- An influx of new hires going through onboarding

- Incorrect estimates

- Poorly planned projects

These problems can be fixed without hiring more people. If you determine that these aren't the cause for the velocity drop, move on to the following list.

- Missing experience and skills

- Burnout due to overwork

- Bottlenecks due to a single person performing too many roles

Unfortunately, these problems aren't fixable without additional hiring or training. Training can alleviate missing skills and bottlenecks over time, but the time it takes varies. Sometimes, the knowledge gap is too large. For example, if your team lacks infrastructure experience and most of the team is junior level, the amount of time needed to learn the many layers before they are confident making changes to AWS will be too great. If you work for a startup, the budget and timeline don't likely exist to support this type of solution.

If the problem is burnout, reducing the team workload can help. If that isn't possible because the company's success relies on too many high-priority projects, you'll need to increase the team size. Expanding the team won't mean an immediate velocity increase. There is a period during onboarding when the new team member is less productive. This is normal, but factoring this into our planning is important. Don't wait until the team is at the breaking point to hire. Use your roadmap to consider when more people will be needed so you can make the transition smooth and painless.

When we decide that hiring is the solution to our problems, we need to proceed carefully. Randomly hiring developers is not a practical approach and leads to problems. We need to be strategic and hire the skills we need. Next, let's delve into how to do this effectively.

Hiring for Need and Not Want

Now that we know we need to increase the team size to meet the company's growing needs, the question is who we hire. The effort and money required to hire a new person are substantial. We do not want to go through the hiring process only to discover we've brought on the wrong type of person.

Let's examine how to identify our needs and focus on the type of hire to make. That way, you can proceed with confidence.

People Doing Too Many Different Jobs

Many teams have a person that others look to for guidance. These individuals, often the most experienced or knowledgeable developers, play a crucial role in the team's success. Their significant contribution is evident in their time assisting rather than coding. They work tirelessly to pace the road for the rest of the team, so their work goes smoothly.

Having people like this on your team isn't in itself a problem. The team benefits from having leaders to push everyone toward a vision or goal. It's one of the reasons why we have strike team leaders.

Issues start when too many of the team are waiting for help from one person. Tasks pile up and go unfinished for multiple sprints. Projects are delayed because our key developer is too busy to review pull requests, design new frameworks, and solve complex problems.

Imagine being that developer handling customer support tickets while performing critical infrastructure changes, all while developing new complex features. Sometimes, there aren't enough hours in the workday to get everything done. At some point, the workload becomes overwhelming, and the whole team suffers as a result. Before this happens, you will need to hire someone who can help the overburdened team member. There may be a temporary dip in productivity during the new hire's training period, but the long-term benefits of shared responsibility will be significant.

Identify Missing Skills

As the application grows in complexity, the skills your team needs change. Building large, scalable web applications requires a different skill set than building a minimal viable product.

Your initial team might be good at quickly creating user-facing features but lack the skills to implement the high availability, serverless computing farm needed to serve millions of users.

With each new milestone, you must reassess your team. Understanding what skills your team needs during that time is key when hiring. Asking yourself some of the following questions can help identify those missing skills.

- What areas of development does the team struggle with?

- What areas of the application have quality issues?

- What parts of the application do developers complain about the most?

- What parts of the application take the longest to develop new features?

Answering these questions helps you zero in on the pain points most likely caused by a lack of skills. You may find more than one missing skill. The following are some of the common skills a new team might lack.

- Infrastructure

- Front end

- Design

- Database administration

- Customer support

- High-scale/high-availability design

Again, most of these skills aren't needed when starting out. The priority is getting the application into a usable state. A point comes where your database size, user traffic, and uptime expectations require specialized skills to handle correctly. If your team doesn't adapt, it will struggle to meet previous velocity numbers.

165

Common Next Hires

As your team grows, the need to hire becomes inevitable. Who you hire depends on your needs. We've already identified these positions. If you are still struggling, however, the following are some typical next hires who could help.

- **Product manager** to plan and manage road mapping and team sprints

- **DevOps** to maintain infrastructure and team tools using scripting and code

- **Front-end developer** to focus on working with front-end frameworks

- **Designer** to handle UI designs and planning of new features

- **Customer success manager** to handle user support and growing user engagement

When starting, the team usually shares the work performed by these roles. However, eventually, the amount of work required for that role becomes too great. Hiring someone full-time to offload the work from the team frees up time to properly focus on their work.

Upgrade Tools

People are a company's number one expense. Increasing team size means more costs and increased management complexity. For these reasons, finding alternative solutions to hiring might be preferable or required depending on your company's budget.

One area we can improve is our tools. When we set up our ecosystem, we picked tools that worked for our budget and needs at the time. Eventually, our needs and tools will change.

For example, maybe you chose Trello as your project management tool because it was easy to understand and provided a free tier. Your team was happy with the simplicity, and it effectively managed your backlog.

Now, your team has grown and is organized into multiple strike teams. You want multiple projects going simultaneously, but Trello doesn't provide the features to do so effectively. The reporting features are lacking, and you can't restrict project access based on teams.

All these problems point to a need for a more feature-rich tool. You might be able to solve the issue with a workaround, but that requires additional time, which you don't have. Switching tools saves you that time, which is better spent on other important tasks.

The project management tool isn't the only tool you may want to upgrade. The following is a list of examples of tools that can save time and money.

- Upgrade to a paid integrated development environment (IDE) to gain access to time-saving features.

- Use tools that analyze code or database performance and provide suggestions.

- Upgrade your GitHub subscription to unlock enhanced features.

- Add or upgrade your observability platform to gain more insight into how your application works in production.

- Migrate from a cheap email to a premier email platform for more features and spam filtering.

- Add a wiki/knowledge base service if using the GitHub ReadMe becomes too tedious.

This isn't a complete list. New tools we haven't thought of will become available after the writing of this book. Artificial intelligence is already changing the way we develop. Who knows what new tools will be available in the future?

One way to determine whether you've outgrown a tool is if you find yourself using it in ways they weren't intended. Also, if you need to do a lot of manual, tedious work to compensate for tool shortcomings, you most likely have outgrown their usefulness.

The effect of switching tools isn't easy to calculate, but you will notice the difference in how your team operates. More projects will get done quicker and on time. Your team will be happier not needing to perform workarounds.

Update Your Process

Upgrading our tools and hiring more people is an effective way to solve velocity problems. This isn't the only way, though. When a team is small and the application is new, the processes we put in place may be barebones. For a team of one, the process might be non-existent. After all, what good is daily standup if there is no one to read it? There is no need for a complicated tool to manage tasks. A to-do list scribbled on a notepad on your desk works just fine. It's when you add more people that your notepad becomes ineffective.

The right amount of process helps promote productivity, improve communication, and, most importantly, prevent bugs. Too much process slows us down, and too little process creates chaos. We want a balance that allows our team to work confidently while not being a burden.

When do we decide to change our process? There are a few ways we can tell that existing processes are insufficient.

- Increase bugs count

- Increased system downtime

- Slower average velocity

- Decreased visibility

When you notice these situations occurring, there might be a process you need to improve. What changes you need depends on the problem. Let's look at some possible issues and how to address them.

Stability

Instability can occur on any team. Poor working dynamics between team members can produce sub-par work. Improper planning can lead to poorly defined tasks, causing developers to misinterpret stories, often guessing the meaning. No one will be satisfied with their output, and morale will suffer.

If you notice problems with your backlog, look at your planning process. If planning is informal, now is the time to formalize it. Make planning meetings a regular occurrence. Involve more people in brainstorming. Introduce a review period, so you have time to iterate on projects. Have your strike team leaders perform a technical review. All these things will improve the quality of the backlog.

The engineering process may need improvement as well. Even the most diligent developer makes mistakes. The benefit of working on a team is that you always have another set of eyes to spot problems. If you don't have a code review process, add one. If you do, consider increasing the number of reviewers for each pull request. Create a checklist of common problems to check for on each review. If you can automate that checklist using a static code analysis library, that's even better. You can have the entire team sign off on release branches before merging to production until production deploys stabilize. Using code pairing can help improve code quality and speed up code reviews.

Keep adding different processes and track the changes. There might be pushback from the team when the changes are first made, but they will come around once they notice the improvements. When the problems go away, you can reevaluate the changes and possibly scale them back.

Management

Keeping the team organized and productive is not easy. If you are struggling to plan and handle day-to-day operations, you may need to add additional processes.

When you begin development, you might choose to skip providing estimates on tasks. However, as the team expands, it becomes increasingly challenging to determine the expected workload per sprint. By adding estimates to all tasks and using project management tool reporting, you can gain valuable insights, making it easier to plan your roadmap. It also helps your team understand expectations and allows them to push back when estimates don't match the actual effort.

Adding labels can make it much easier to identify the type of tasks in the backlog. Red labels for blocked tasks can provide a visual indication of possible problems. Adding additional lanes to the planning board can provide finer-grained control over visualizing task state. Keep adding and trying different ideas until managing your team gets easier. Now, let's talk about making changes without creating too many waves.

Making a Change

When the time comes to make a change, we want to avoid interrupting the development progress. Before deciding, discuss your plans with your team and gather feedback. They might have insight into the problem you aren't aware of. The decision of how to run the team is ultimately yours, but feedback is always welcome. You can't make everyone happy with your decision, but including your team makes them feel heard and prevents you from missing something. You can also make more minor changes to lessen the likelihood of pushback. A bunch of small changes over time are easier to digest than big ones.

If you need to move to a new tool or make significant process changes, give time for your team to learn about the change before implementing it. You can do this independently or together as a group study. After implementing the change, don't panic at the drop in velocity while the team adapts. Eventually, velocity will return to normal once the team gets comfortable, hopefully surpassing past numbers.

If you are hiring an additional developer, determine which strike team they will join or if they are forming their own. As a general rule, limit a strike team to three to four developers. This size limit prevents the strike team leader from being overwhelmed.

If you hire a developer and there isn't a strike team available to join, you have a couple of options.

- Promote a mid-level developer to a senior level and make them a strike team leader.

- Temporarily add the developer to a strike team that is already at the limit.

Ideally, when a strike team has reached a threshold, we build a new strike team, hiring the senior developer first and then filling out the team. However, this doesn't always work out, so be flexible. Nothing is permanent, and you can always change your mind. If productivity stays high over the long term, everyone is happy.

Summary

We've worked through several ways to handle growth and change. It may come in the form of new hires, tool upgrades, and process modifications. When encountering problems, it might be tempting to resist change because making changes slows us down. These dips in productivity are ultimately rewarded. Don't wait until the problem gets so bad that it damages your team's long-term productivity.

Hiring more developers is cheaper than losing your existing team due to burnout and potential business loss. Spending more money on a tool is more affordable than hiring a developer. As you continue to make changes, you begin to understand when change is needed.

CHAPTER 9

Building a Community

One aspect of an in-person work environment that people miss when working on a remote team is the connections they build with their co-workers. Outside of friends and family, our co-workers are the people we spend the most time with. It's no wonder people often form friendships or lifelong work relationships with these people. These connections are built slowly through little interactions throughout the workday. This face-to-face time allows us to get to know them better, whether it's impromptu meetings at the breakroom coffee station or group lunches.

On a remote team, we can go days without seeing or talking to our team. When deep in a sprint, we post a daily standup, read through any posted by our team, and move on with our day. Once the workday is complete, you shut the laptop and disconnect.

While some may appreciate remote work's break from forced social interactions, isolation can lead to a feeling of detachment for others. When this isolation worsens, the people we work with become nothing more than text messages and emails attached to a profile picture. This loss of team connection can significantly impact team dynamics and productivity.

When working remotely, team interactions become sensitive. A poorly worded comment in a pull request might be taken as an insult. We can be quick to anger when working with old code, not understanding the circumstances under which it was created. We want to avoid these uncomfortable situations and provide an environment rich with interactions, just like an in-person workplace.

C. DiLeo and J. Reyes, *Effective Remote Teams*,
https://doi.org/10.1007/979-8-8688-1303-0_9

This chapter discusses ways to replace the social interactions lost when working remotely. We use our tools to create opportunities for the team to interact. We build personal connections through regular face-to-face interactions. Let's start by providing a way to encourage small, short interactions that offer glimpses into our co-workers' lives outside of work.

Virtual Water Cooler

The water cooler became the icon of the American breakroom in the late twentieth century. With its shiny white or black plastic bottom and transparent cylinder jug of water placed on top, it became more than a place to get a drink. It symbolizes casual work conversations.

Thirsty? Take a walk to the breakroom and pull a cup of water. Who knows which co-worker you'll bump into? Talk about the weekend or share updates on family life. It didn't matter what you talked about or how long the conversation was. The water cooler was the meeting place.

For those in the tech industry, the past two decades have witnessed a transformation of the water cooler into something grander. Unlimited snacks, specialty coffees, and fun distractions like video games have become the norm. Even smaller companies have had to adapt, adding extra perks to keep up with the changing landscape.

All of it provided additional time to socialize at work. We will never be able to replicate this level of community on a remote team, but there are several things we can do to try. This section provides different ideas for you to try. Which ones work depends on your team.

Non-Work Real-Time Chat Channel

Real-time chat allows us to create any number of channels. Work channels provide a steady stream of work-related conversation. Occasionally, these conversations may veer off course, but I should mostly stay focused on work.

Creating non-work channels provides a place for people to talk about whatever they like, within reason, of course. By creating channels around shared interests, we give our team a chance to share and discover things about each other.

It's important to create channels that cover topics that aren't considered sensitive. Controversial topics can quickly devolve into arguments or discussions people aren't comfortable with. It's best to play it safe and avoid these potential HR situations.

Instead, focus on common interests. Ask your team for a list of their interests to get some ideas. Here are some ideas to get you started.

- Coffee
- Pets
- Video games
- Books
- Outdoors activities
- Travel
- Food

New channels are created as you discover more about your team. Don't hold back when adding new channels. You can remove old ones when they become stale. If someone on the team isn't interested in a topic, they can mute or leave the channel.

Coffee Chat

Every time you hire a new team member, have them set up 30-minute one-on-one meetings with each person on the team. You can even extend this to the entire company if it is small enough. There is no agenda for this meeting. Grab a drink of choice—coffee, tea, or water—and talk about anything. Your company can even pay for the drink through a reimbursement or voucher.

The main objective of these meetings is to provide a dedicated time for your team to bond by getting to know each other. By creating these informal opportunities, you're helping to foster more connections.

Space out these meetings over several weeks to avoid burnout. Joining a team can be overwhelming. The amount of information a new hire takes in the first few weeks is intense. Give time for each meeting to sink in before moving on to the next.

Non-Work Team Meetings

In addition to one-on-one meetings, scheduling regular meetings where your team discusses non-work topics can help foster community. These 30-minute to one-hour meetings have no agenda or structure, but adding an activity for everyone to participate in, like a game, can help break the ice.

Schedule a recurring event in your shared calendar with a link to a video conference room. Suggest that everyone enable their video, but don't make it mandatory. You want to remove barriers so that the team wants to join and feel encouraged to participate. Not having the pressure to be on video sometimes encourages a person to enable it.

Schedule the meeting during business hours, and if the funds are available, you can re-reimburse or provide gift cards for food. On bigger teams, you can split the meetings per strike team if time zones are an issue. Also, having video chats with fewer people means more soft-spoken team members will be inclined to contribute.

In-Person Co-Working

Running a remote team doesn't always mean your team is disturbed worldwide. Even though your team works remotely, everyone may still live relatively close to one another.

If this is the case, consider hosting regular in-person working meetups. Gather at a coffee shop, library, or co-working space for half a day to a full day. Let your team set the agenda for the meetup. Whether they work quietly or collaborate as a group, this time is valuable for building connections. Offer for the company to buy the first cup of coffee. It's an inexpensive way to entice people to show up.

Make this meetup optional. Ideally, have people RSVP to the calendar event. This helps others decide whether to attend.

Office Hours

Flexibility is one of the benefits of working remotely. Depending on your rules, the team has the power to choose where and when they work. Because the team can work from anywhere, approaching you with concerns and questions isn't as easy as approaching you in your office.

Knowing when others will be at their computers and online is hard in a remote environment. Sometimes, you end up playing tag with them, going offline as they come online, and vice versa. We need a predictable way for the team to get in touch with you when needed, which we accomplish using video conferencing. By starting a video meeting at predetermined times during the week and staying logged in even when no one has joined, we provide an informal way for the team to get in contact.

People can join the video call for any reason. They might need to ask work-related questions or talk about something personal. What's important is not what they want to talk about but that you are available for them regularly.

Determine once or twice weekly that you can sit on a video conference call with an open invite. If the team is large, ask your strike team leaders to do the same but limit their office hours to once per week. During this time, continue to work as you normally would, but with the caveat that it may be interrupted when someone joins.

Company Off-Site

Regularly bringing the entire company together in the same location can refocus everyone and provide bonding time. This time spent together can be a powerful motivator. Seeing all your co-workers together talking about the company's next steps is a reminder that the company is real.

Interacting in person with co-workers helps us build empathy. During the daily grind of work, it's easy to forget there are people on the other side of the real-time chat messages. Spending extended periods together helps lower guards and opens people to sharing. When we learn more about the people we work with, it provides context to the work they produce.

Instead of jumping to a negative conclusion when encountering an obvious flaw in the code, we might consider the person behind that flaw. After all, it's very rare that a developer intentionally writes bad code. Often, a story is associated with the bad code we don't see. Maybe they were sick or under an extremely tight schedule. Sometimes, it's a simple mistake caused by a lack of knowledge. Whatever the cause, without one-on-one time with our co-workers, we have no context.

Agenda

How often you get the team together depends on several factors, but the main issue is money. Depending on your company's size and distribution, getting everyone to the same location can be costly. Bigger teams cost more and, therefore, need to get together less frequently.

You need to decide what works best for your situation. If possible, we recommend meeting every six months. If that frequency isn't possible, we recommend meeting at least once a year.

What the company does during the off-site is up to you. Ideally, we want the activities to blend work and socializing. Having the entire company together provides valuable opportunities for collaboration and planning. Also, making time for non-work activities gives everyone time to talk without work-related stress.

The following is an example agenda for your off-site.

- **Company update**: Prepare updates from each department. Share what has been completed since your last off-site. Discuss the plan for the next six months or so. Celebrate and acknowledge achievements. If there are any problems or hurdles the company must overcome in the future, share them and allow everyone to ask questions.

- **In-person work session**: Provide time for teams to split up and work together. There doesn't need to be a particular goal during this time. Each team may decide to build prototypes, have technical discussions, or work silently.

- **Activities**: Leave time for fun activities. These can be as elaborate or as simple as you can afford. Remember that your company is made up of different types of personalities. What one person finds fun might be stressful for another. Try picking activities that accommodate everyone.

- **Downtime**: Allow the company to hang out in a common space like a coffee shop, arcade, or co-working space. Don't make this time mandatory. Provide the space, let everyone know when, and let things happen naturally.

Planning an off-site is a lot of work, but what you gain from this time is invaluable. You might be tempted to fill the off-site from beginning to end with nonstop events. Remember, the off-site isn't meant to be a party. It's a chance for all the employees to spend quality time together. Find a balance between productivity, fun, and downtime. We want the team to leave the off-site invigorated, not burned out.

From the Top Down

Much of company culture comes from the top and trickles down. The people running the company can spend all the time they want trying to create the ideal company culture, but if they don't live by it, their efforts will be in vain.

If managers don't take lunch breaks and eat at their desks, their direct reports will do the same. This continues down the organizational ladder until it's an unspoken rule everyone abides by. Suddenly, no one wants to be the one person who actually takes advantage of their complete lunch break.

Imagine being hired at a company, and the hiring manager highlights the company's extensive sick leave, underlining their dedication to employee health. On your first day, your manager is working regardless of being ill. When you ask why they didn't take a sick day, they say they can't because of a deadline. A month later, the CEO attends your company's all-hands meeting from vacation. You will think twice about using a sick day or scheduling paid time off.

If you want your company to promote a balanced work/life environment, the ones in charge must embody it. When the CEO utilizes their paid time off and vocalizes it to the entire company, the middle management will do the same, followed by the individual contributors.

An open-door policy is another workplace standard popular within the tech industry. Having a company where employees feel safe sharing their opinions and concerns means that management needs to share constantly.

They can share company financials or highlight successes and failures during company meetings. When management shares the good with the bad, everyone at the company is more likely to do the same.

Smaller updates can be shared on the general real-time chat channel. Sharing on the general channel allows everyone to comment and ask questions.

CHAPTER 9   BUILDING A COMMUNITY

You and your strike team leaders can share successes and highlight developers with the company. Being open about planned or unplanned outages can build transparency in the company's development process. Often, employees outside of engineering need to be made aware of the intricacies of creating software. Sharing problems, their causes, and the fixes can provide insight into all the hard work that goes into creating a stable system. As your software improves, everyone can observe the stability improve in real-time vs. being hidden behind a curtain.

Summary

Building a community takes time and effort but is worth the investment. Working remotely can provide a level of flexibility and freedom not possible in an in-person environment. However, it can also be a very isolating experience.

Providing virtual spaces for the team to communicate is essential. It gives them time to build camaraderie and reminds them they are part of a team. Making leadership available from top to bottom makes the company feel open and safe to explore new ideas. Getting everyone together regularly provides face-to-face time that builds connections. All of this is vital to erasing the boundaries created by remote work. If we keep at it, the team feels as connected as when working in person.

CHAPTER 10

Longevity

No team remains the same forever. There are many reasons a team grows and shrinks. When your company experiences periods of success, you'll need more people to help with the increased workload. When there are hardships, letting people go might be necessary to keep the company afloat. Sometimes, people leave regardless of company finances. All of this is part of running a business.

Long gone are the days when employees committed 30 years to a single company. Layoffs have become a standard business strategy to improve fiscal quarter earnings, and benefits like pensions have all but disappeared. There isn't much incentive to stay in one job for long. As a result, workers end up switching jobs often. Most developers remain at a job for less than two years. (Zippia)[1]

Who can blame them? When there is no benefit to staying in one place, why stay? It's better to cut ties with a company before you're laid off unexpectedly. This is a big problem for a manager who wants to build a productive, stable team. Dealing with constant turnover is expensive and time-consuming. Every time a team member leaves, you lose institutional knowledge that sets your team and company back, sometimes permanently.

While we can't force people not to leave, there is a lot we can do to encourage them to stay. This chapter examines why people choose to go. Then, we lay out our plan to improve our odds of keeping developers for the long haul.

---

[1] https://www.zippia.com/software-engineer-jobs/demographics/.

© Carleton DiLeo, Jennifer Reyes 2025
C. DiLeo and J. Reyes, *Effective Remote Teams*,
https://doi.org/10.1007/979-8-8688-1303-0_10

Why Do They Leave

Work is a significant part of life. We work to provide for ourselves and our families. We spend so much of our lives at work that, understandably, some people will want that time to be worth the long hours. Whether maximizing our hourly wage or having a job we don't hate, everyone wants the best possible job.

This section explores several reasons why people change jobs. These reasons aren't in any particular order. Someone could leave a team for one or more of these reasons. Understanding them is the first step before countering them with meaningful action.

Better Pay

The first reason people leave is probably the most obvious. Offers of a higher salary can make a person question their current compensation. The higher the jump in pay, the more likely they are to consider the offer.

Since we work to earn a living, the more we earn, the more we can afford and save. Developers, especially those early in their careers, can see wage increases in the double-digit percentage range when jumping to a new job. With the rise in remote job positions, workers aren't limited to their geographic region, significantly increasing opportunity. Developers can easily find companies willing to pay them more, especially in cities with high competition.

Better Work/Life Balance

Money is important, but it isn't everything. There comes a point when we make enough to support ourselves comfortably. Anything beyond that point is icing on the cake. With more money, we can save more and afford nicer vacations, but what then? What happens when those increased wages come at a personal cost?

A high salary paired with lengthy, grueling hours may not be worth it. Some developers with families may find the long hours incompatible with their lives. Starting work before their kids wake up and ending work after they go to bed isn't sustainable. There becomes a point when the sacrifice isn't worth the extra money.

For people without families, there are other ways long hours might be incompatible with their lives. Living an active, healthy life requires time for exercise, sleep, and a balanced diet. Maintaining relationships with loved ones means attending birthdays and get-togethers. This becomes nearly impossible during periods of crunch.

There is a limit to what people can handle. Poor planning and resource management inevitably pushes a team to the limit. When you push your team too hard, they eventually look elsewhere for a better job.

No Career Path

Landing your first software development job is an exciting time. All the studying and training have finally paid off, and you get a chance to write code professionally. The first year or two can fly by. Your skills improve at an exponential rate during this period. It's easy to lose track of time when caught up in all the excitement.

At some point, you look up from your computer and ask what's next. Instead of only coding, you have ideas on system design and interests outside your current role. If there is no path forward, boredom sets in.

It's easy to forget that people don't want to do the same job forever. As their managers, we must constantly challenge them, give them more responsibility, increase their salary, and work with them to earn a promotion. If there is nothing for your developers to work toward, they will feel there is no future for them at the company. They update their résumé, and the search begins for someone willing to give them the opportunity they deserve.

Newer, Shinier

Technology is constantly changing. Even though CPU speeds and memory are no longer doubling every six months, writing software looks much different than it did a decade ago. Advances in web browsers have made front-end applications more sophisticated. New languages are frequently released, providing the next evolution in productivity and speed. Expanding cloud service offerings makes launching and scaling a web application easier.

During the setup phase, the choices available to you can be overwhelming. Making the right decision is a balancing act of considering the latest trends while knowing when it's okay to use what you're already comfortable with. Sometimes, using a newer technology can mean access to a better feature set, which increases productivity. Other times, using an older, more established technology allows you to leverage years of existing open-source libraries and a pool of developers with a deep understanding of the platform.

As developers, we are naturally drawn to the allure of new technologies. The thrill of exploring the unknown and uncovering hidden surprises is part of our DNA. This same curiosity fuels our problem-solving abilities but can also lead us astray. If we attempt to adopt every new technology that piques our interest, we risk falling into a perpetual cycle of experimentation, hindering our progress and productivity.

Like everything in software development, there needs to be a balance. If we stay too rooted in the past, we may miss significant advancements that can improve our application's stability, performance, and scalability. We can miss new methodologies that will enhance our team's productivity and ability to deliver a quality product.

Imagine being a team that ignored Agile and instead stuck to waterfall methodology. What if your team decides to skip version control systems like Git or migrate to a modern programming language with memory management? Some of these choices might sound ridiculous in hindsight, but when these technologies and practices came out, people weren't immediately convinced they should adopt them. If a team was stubborn enough, it could be years before they even consider it an option. A developer wanting to move forward but being held back by their team only lasts so long.

Staying too rooted in the past is also dangerous for the company. Newer companies adopt these technologies and practices, utilizing them to gain an advantage, eventually overtaking your company and acquiring your users. Developers on your team will worry about their skills becoming obsolete. They'll start looking elsewhere for a place where their skills won't stagnate.

More Exciting Work

Regardless of our passion for our job, some days fly by while others cease to end. No matter the job, we are sometimes assigned tasks we don't want to do. We do them anyway because it's our job. That doesn't mean we don't dream of more exciting work while we do it.

As mentioned, developers are drawn to work that stimulates their brains. Whether we are faced with complex problems or new technology, we want our jobs to challenge us. Some developers are drawn to working on products they use regularly.

Whatever the reason, a bored developer is an unhappy developer. They are likely to spend their spare time browsing job listings. Even if they initially enjoyed their work, the novelty could wear off. The developer won't stick around for long if the manager doesn't recognize this.

Frustrating Code

We've talked about technical debt in previous chapters. We incur technical debt from poor choices during development. Over time, they accumulate and make our application slow and brittle. If this debt isn't repaid through refactoring, bugs will overwhelm the team. There becomes a point where the code is too difficult to work with. If nothing changes, your developers will look elsewhere for a team that values quality.

The effects of technical debt aren't felt immediately. Therefore, it can be difficult to know exactly where they came from. There are parts of your code that the team is afraid to modify. Deploying to production feels like a gamble. Finishing projects on time becomes a hit or miss.

The more time developers spend in this environment, the more jaded they become. Pretending everything is okay and pushing forward in the name of "just getting it done" only worsens the situation. The team suffers as a result. The culture slowly shifts to one that isn't focused on quality. The team becomes less invested in the product and looks for other places where their time would be better spent.

Team Is Not a Good Fit

Some developers are loud and opinionated, voicing their ideas at every meeting. Others are quiet and like to carefully consider their options before saying anything. Some are passionate about new technologies, while others prefer to stick with what they are used to.

These different personalities don't always work well together. Quiet developers may feel like their voices aren't heard, while the vocal ones may feel they are doing all the work. No matter how good a team looks on paper, progress will be slow if they can't work together, and the result won't be ideal.

Not everyone you want to hire will be a good fit. Someone's skills might be the exact match for the position, or they have decades of experience you want to leverage. But it won't work out if they don't get along with the team.

Getting Them to Stay

When you hire a new developer, their excitement for the new job has peaked. All the preparations and interviews have gotten them a foot in the door and crossed the finish line into a new world of opportunity. Reality slowly sets in, and the new job becomes just another with its own set of pros and cons. This is a natural progression for many things in life and not necessarily a bad thing. It's what keeps us striving for the next milestone. It becomes a problem when the excitement dips so low that it becomes complacency.

We must always look for ways to challenge our team and provide them with reasonable compensation for their work. Finding a balance allows them to excel and makes them want to stay longer. This section introduces ways to keep your team engaged and hopefully employed.

Benefits

Compensation and benefits are major reasons people decide to stay or leave a job. It makes sense; everyone wants to be paid as much as possible for their time. If they make more, they can live more securely and afford more.

Sometimes, your company can't afford to pay top dollar. You don't need to hit the top end of the salary range, but you'll need to come close enough to the fair market pay for comparable skills. If you hire at a low wage, even a junior developer eventually becomes experienced and skilled enough to demand more money. If you don't oblige them with a higher salary, they will find a company that will.

Incremental pay increases every year can help keep a person's pay competitive. While more money is a direct solution, other ways exist to compensate employees.

Benefits like generous paid time off, stock options, low-cost healthcare, parental leave, and a 401k with matching are all creative ways to entice employees to stay.

There are other options other than the standard benefits that are worth considering.

- Stipend for a home office
- Yearly stipend for continued learning (books, conferences, training, etc.)
- High-end company-provided equipment
- Monthly stipend for co-working space, parking, or coffee to allow working from somewhere other than home
- Pay for employee-requested tools and software
- Stipend for gym membership

These benefits make employees feel appreciated because the company is willing to go above and beyond their standard compensation to keep them happy.

If you are willing to be even more creative, some benefits don't have a direct cost but can be very valuable to employees. These require us to think beyond the typical work environment.

- Flexible work hours
- Less than 40-hour workweek
- Four-day workweek
- Paid sabbaticals

These might be harder to get approval on if you're not the one running the company. For most companies, the accepted convention is to work nine to five and five days per week. Forty hours is the minimum commitment for employees, while some companies ask salary employees to work more. Having a cap of 40 hours per week can also be an incentive for many people in our field.

Providing the option for flexible hours can be more for developers than working whenever they want. Software development is a thought job that requires a lot of mental energy to execute well. Writing code isn't a repetitive task where developers type nonstop for eight hours. Solving problems takes time and involves a lot of discussion and contemplation. Sometimes, hours of thought can go into even the most minor changes. Allowing developers to choose when they work enables them to form a schedule that maximizes productivity.

Another option is requiring less than 40 hours of work per week. It gives developers time for other things in their lives and enables them to justify a lower salary.

One final idea to consider is allowing the team to work a four-day workweek. The extra day would give developers an extended weekend to recover and come back to work refreshed.

These benefits are rare among companies and can give you an edge. Once a developer is used to these perks, giving them up can be challenging, making it harder for them to leave, which is what you want.

Defined Career Path

Having a defined career path makes progress in the company concrete. It removes doubt about where each developer is in their career and where they will be in a certain amount of time. Job hierarchies provide management with an easy way to track each employee's progress and are helpful when hiring.

Start by examining each job type you need or currently have on the team. Consider the lowest experience level of that job type and the top. Don't worry about the job types you don't need at the moment. You can add those hierarchies when it's time to hire for that position.

Let's say you've hired a senior developer and a mid-level developer. The possible career progression for that job type can look like this.

Junior Software Engineer

—> Software Engineer

—> Senior Software Engineer

—> Staff Software Engineer

—> Principal Software Engineer

Since the software industry has mainly formalized around naming, you can look at job postings for ideas if you need help to think of a good hierarchy. If you plan to hire a product or DevOps team, create a similar hierarchy for those positions. Also, as the team grows, middle management becomes necessary. As a result, you'll also need a hierarchy for these jobs.

You can make changes later if needed, but make sure these changes are communicated with your team beforehand. If the change will alter people's positions in the hierarchy, take the time to talk with each person so it's clear where they fit in.

Depending on the requirements for each level, a career progression may define a 10- to 15-year journey for someone starting at the bottom and working their way to the top. Considering the average time a developer spends at one company, this is enough for most developers to feel there is significant room for growth.

Next, you'll need to define the details for each level. Be specific. Provide as much detail as possible while also leaving some room for interpretation. We want what is required for a promotion to be clear but leave room for people to be ready for the next level sooner than others. Provide ranges instead of explicit requirements.

Next, let's look at each aspect of a job description.

Years of Experience

Here, we define the year of professional working experience. You want to specify years of experience with specific technologies or performing a certain job function. Remember to provide a range rather than a discrete number. For example, a senior software engineer may require three to five years of general programming experience and two to three years working with a specific technology stack.

A range allows for flexibility. Some developer's skills progress faster than others. Holding back a promotion because they don't meet a fixed number of years of experience can mean losing them to another company. Don't make the range too large. And avoid overlapping with other job descriptions.

Responsibility

Here, we describe the responsibilities of the position. For example, a junior developer spends time writing well-tested code that does not cause production bugs. A senior developer designs new frameworks and leads projects. The responsibilities for each position should match the experience and skills outlined in the previous section.

These serve as a guide when working toward promotion. A developer should learn how to perform the responsibilities by shadowing a more experienced developer and, afterward, perform these responsibilities themselves. This approach allows the developer to receive formal training and for you to see how they handle the new responsibilities.

The list of responsibilities also acts as a template for a job listing when hiring new people. Ideally, you should be able to copy and paste the responsibility section of the job details and place it in the job description.

Role on the Team

Unless you are at the top of a company organizational chart, you report to someone. Your boss ensures your work is satisfactory and handles your HR-related concerns. They make decisions about your career growth at the company, but other decision-making hierarchies exist on a team. Specific roles on your team have responsibilities that make them points of contact for certain decisions.

A senior software engineer may not be another software engineer's boss. Still, if they are a strike team leader, they have the final say on their team's technical decisions and task allocation.

Continuing up the ladder, a staff software engineer isn't a senior software engineer's boss, but they play a key role in providing technical guidance across multiple teams. They review designs and understand how each component fits into the project's bigger picture. They can override a strike team leader's decision if they disagree with a technical detail.

This goes up the ladder to the top, wherever that may be for your structure. Each level of the job hierarchy should look to the next level for guidance. Every level should have a role that decides what decisions they are authorized to make.

One-on-Ones

Problems with our team don't happen suddenly; they build over time until they finally spill over. Some people will vocalize their concerns, but many will not. Far too often, developers continue to plug away at their work and chalk up problems as something they must deal with.

These problems range from small, fixable issues like overly long meetings to deep-rooted problems like pay inequality and career stagnation. Most of the time, when a developer finally decides to speak up about deep-rooted problems, it's probably too late. They're already looking for better opportunities. Luckily, regular check-ins can mitigate most of these issues. As long as we take measurable action to improve problems as they arise, the team will respond in kind.

Set up weekly or bi-weekly meetings with every team member. If your team is too big to manage, delegate these meetings to other managers. Have them handle one-on-ones with direct reports, bubbling up any problems they can't handle to you.

These meetings should have a set agenda where you discuss the following with your team.

- **Previous week(s)**
  - Issues with other team members
  - Issues preventing them from doing their job
  - Issues with the company
- **Coming week(s)**
  - What they should expect with future tasking
  - Any role changes that will occur
  - Changes in team structure or team growth and shrinkage
- **Career progression**
  - Any goals that have been met or partially met
  - Problems with the progression
  - Action items to get them over hurdles
- **Future work**
  - Important future projects
  - Future opportunities like leading a project or working with new technology

Leave the meeting with action items and return to them in the following meeting. Set deadlines for the action items. The more formal these meetings are, the easier it is to understand when there is a problem.

Regularly listening to each team member lets you fix problems before they become more significant. These meetings help you understand which people work well together and which do not. You also better understand each person's strengths and weaknesses. If you have multiple teams, this information can help you move people to different teams which might be a better fit. Finally, it allows you to understand your shortcomings when multiple team members report similar issues.

No Pigeonholing

Developers like to explore and learn new things. We are not always the best at sharing these discoveries, even within our team. Each person brings different experiences and skills to a company, which can make some more qualified to work on tasks using a specific technology. That's to be expected, and playing to people's strengths might be necessary when you're under a time crunch. Left unchecked, this can quickly become a problem. You've probably worked on a team with a "database person" or the "bug fixer." These are the go-to people for specific tasks or parts of the application. Others overutilize them for their knowledge and expertise.

What happens when that person goes on vacation or quits? Who does the team go to now? Pigeonholing a person into a particular role often prevents them from doing anything else. Sometimes, it can make planning time off impossible. It won't be long before they've had enough and start looking for another job.

To combat this, make it part of your team culture to always share knowledge or write documentation. You can have weekly team share meetings where someone teaches the team how to perform a task or use a piece of technology. Placing knowledge on an internal wiki allows developers to help themselves when there are questions rather than waiting for help.

If someone on your team performs a menial task every week, automate it. Anything you can do to give that person back hours of their week will free them up for newer, more exciting work. This not only helps retain that person but also allows the team to improve. Share often, automate repetitive tasks, and document everything.

Technology

We don't always need to work with the latest and greatest technology to be productive and happy. Often, being on the bleeding edge means a lot of pain—that's why it's called the "bleeding" edge, after all. Yet, we also don't want our skills to become stagnant or our applications become susceptible to exploits.

We want a balance that keeps us moving forward while not bogged down in dealing with non-production-ready software. Create a plan to update your current technology stack regularly. Apply security patches immediately, update to point releases within a time frame, and make major release upgrades part of a quarterly or yearly schedule. Allow the team time to review new features and foster discussions. Use tools like Dependabot on GitHub to automate and build updates into your process. Linters are also valuable tools for informing you of deprecated features or helping you learn new syntax.

Whatever you do, don't ignore the advancements in your chosen platform. Staying informed rewards you with improved stability and performance and keeps your team engaged with the work.

When new technology is released, like languages or frameworks, allow the team to investigate the ones they are interested in. Have them perform spikes where they can build prototypes to learn the basics. You don't have to use what's created; we encourage you to treat the code written as disposable. What you are looking for is knowledge. The team will learn new ways of approaching problems and a new piece of technology to their toolset for future projects.

We aren't saying you should abandon your current platform on a whim. After all, the web framework you picked is likely sufficient for most of your team's needs. There is always the possibility that you will have a need that goes outside of the bounds of what your framework or language supports. Using another technology can save a lot of time and money. When you aren't fighting with your tools to make something work, the result is much better and easier to maintain. Also, if your team ignores all other advances in your field, they won't know what's available. If they don't know a better tool is available, there's no way to consider if it's viable.

Experimenting with new technology can also be mentally satisfying for a team. Using the same language and frameworks can become dull over time, no matter how shiny and new they once were. Letting developers explore new technology allows their skills to grow and satisfy the curiosity that might pull them away from the team.

Continued Learning

Developers are always learning. We learn new methodologies, languages, frameworks, patterns, and so on—the list is never-ending and part of the job. Without this endless quest for knowledge, we become bored and complacent. Writing code becomes a repetitive task akin to data entry.

Making learning a part of your culture is important to keeping the team engaged. Providing perks that encourage learning is a good way to start. Offer a stipend to buy books, pay for the team to attend local conferences, and give subscriptions to platforms with video courses. Most of these options are affordable and will repay the company with the new skills acquired.

Have the team engage in shared weekly learning sessions. Watch recorded conference talks, form a book club, and have experienced developers share knowledge. If you make learning a regular, recurring part of work, the team is more likely to engage.

As we promote a culture of learning, we reduce the likelihood of developers feeling they are missing out on new skills. Left unchecked, these feelings of doubt can lead to developers exploring job opportunities elsewhere.

Summary

This chapter examined what makes people consider leaving your team for better jobs. While many of the reasons we covered can lead a developer astray, often, it's an accumulation of any of these problems that causes them to leave.

The chapter also explored how to entice people to stay. Paying a fair wage is a start, but we can employ many other options to make leaving difficult. We aim to make developers feel they would lose more than they gain by switching jobs.

If you are committed, you can build a remote team that improves over time and creates a product the company is proud of.

Index

H, I, J, K

L

M, N

GPSR Compliance
The European Union's (EU) General Product Safety Regulation (GPSR) is a set
of rules that requires consumer products to be safe and our obligations to
ensure this.

If you have any concerns about our products, you can contact us on

ProductSafety@springernature.com

In case Publisher is established outside the EU, the EU authorized
representative is:

Springer Nature Customer Service Center GmbH
Europaplatz 3
69115 Heidelberg, Germany